PROOFREADING & EDITING BUSINESS DOCUMENTS

Second Edition

Patricia E. Seraydarian, Ph.D.

PARADIGM

Consulting Editor: Marjorie Lisovskis
Cover Designer: Queue Publishing Services
Text Designer: Korman Design Services
Composition: Mori Studio
Illustrator: Jorel Williams

Acknowledgment
Thank you to the following consultant for her valuable
contribution in reviewing this book:
Paula Campbell, Curriculum Specialist, Irvine, California.

Library of Congress Cataloging-in-Publication Data
Seraydarian, Patricia E.
    Proofreading & editing business documents/Patricia E.
Seraydarian. — 2d ed.
        p.   cm.
    Includes index.
    ISBN 1-56118-581-7
    1. Business writing. 2. Proofreading. 3. Editing. I. Title.
II. Title: Proofreading and editing business documents.
HF5718.3.S438   1995
651.7'4—dc20   94-35560
                                                CIP

© 1996 by Paradigm Publishing Inc.
        Published by EMCParadigm
        875 Montreal Way
        St. Paul, Minnesota 55102
        (800)-328-1452
        www.emcp.com
        E-mail: educate@emcp.com

Printed in the United States of America.
10 9 8 7 6 5 4

TABLE OF CONTENTS

*W*hile technology has simplified the preparation of business documents, it has not relieved us of the responsibility of proofreading to ensure that documents are correct. The very speed with which documents can be produced accentuates the need for careful proofreading.

Just what is proofreading? *Proofreading* is comparing a keyed document against an original (or source) document and checking the keyed document for accuracy and correctness.

Proofreading involves the ability to locate and correct three types of errors: (1) format errors or inconsistencies, (2) typographical errors, and (3) meaning, or content, errors. This text is designed to help you develop your proofreading skill to the mastery level.

Unit I emphasizes proofreading techniques for short business documents including letters, memos, agendas, news releases, and minutes of meetings.

Unit II emphasizes techniques for longer business documents. These documents include business reports, front and end matter of reports, and special parts sometimes included in business reports.

Unit III addresses the proofreading of graphic-oriented pages or documents, containing tables and charts. This unit also includes proofreading techniques for envelopes and labels.

Unit IV integrates light editing functions often associated with proofreading responsibilities.

Each chapter in this text focuses on proofreading techniques for a specific document type. Each document type requires a different approach to proofreading if format, typographic, and context errors are to be located and corrected.

Every chapter opens with a presentation of specific techniques for locating format errors and inconsistencies. This is followed by a second section emphasizing language skills to assist you in ensuring that the document is grammatically correct. The third section of each chapter assesses your skills in proofreading authentic business documents.

Throughout the text, reference aids and checklists summarize key proofreading strategies and skills. Formatting Checkpoints provide guidelines for formatting different types of documents. Proofreading Pointers and Proofreading Alerts point out areas needing special attention. As you begin, it may seem difficult to remember all the details of format, usage, and spelling. However, as you become more experienced at proofreading, these will become second nature to you.

As all of the learnings come together throughout the text, you will feel your confidence in your own proofreading ability grow. You will be aware that you are well on the way to becoming a "master proofreader."

Formatting checkpoints provide guidelines for formatting different types of documents. Proofreading Pointers and Proofreading Alerts point out areas needing special attention.

PROOFREADERS' MARKS
AN INTRODUCTION

Proofreaders' marks, used to indicate corrections, are a universal language for everyone who works with text or graphic documents. Thus, originators, reviewers, word processors, desktop publishers, and printers all understand the marks and the proposed changes they represent.

The most common proofreaders' marks are introduced. You will first study their applications through sample documents. Then, you will use the Proofreader's Cue Card (located at the back of the text) to apply them to a short business document. By the time you complete the applications in this text, you will feel very confident in using proofreaders' marks on your own documents. Use the following procedure to learn them:

1. Study each mark, its meaning, and the example.
2. Compare the proofread copy of the sample document with the final copy to see how the marks were applied.

PROOFREADERS' MARKS

Mark	Meaning	Example	Corrected
‖	Align vertically	‖ A positive attitude makes the day go faster.	A positive attitude makes the day go faster.
⌒⌣	Close up	over head projector	overhead projector
—e (or) ℓ	Delete text	Maria and and Juan / commitment	Maria and Juan / commitment
——	Delete and replace text	will / I shall plan to do so.	I will plan to do so.
⌇⌇	Delete justification	Your job interview is next⌇⌇ Monday at 2:30 p.m.⌇⌇	Your job interview is next Monday at 2:30 p.m.
SS | DS | TS	Correct line spacing (single space, double space, triple space)	SS | employers, employees, and consultants	employers, employees, and consultants
⊏	Move left	⊏ after the meeting	after the meeting
⊐	Move right	1.BASIC / 2. FORTRAN / 3. Assembly	1. BASIC / 2. FORTRAN / 3. Assembly
⟨⟩↲	Move text	She only mailed it yesterday.	She mailed it only yesterday.
#	New paragraph	# Your report is due.	Your report is due.
no #	No paragraph	The check is in the mail. / no # Please call me when you receive it.	The check is in the mail. Please call me when you receive it.
⊐⊏	Center	⊐ Agenda ⊏	Agenda
∧	Insert text	new / the person ∧	the new person
⌄	Insert punctuation	phones, tapes and TVs	phones, tapes, and TVs
#	Insert space	# / phones tapes, and TVs	phones, tapes, and TVs
——	Underline	Requirement #1	Requirement #1

Some proofreaders' marks that use margin notations are illustrated here.

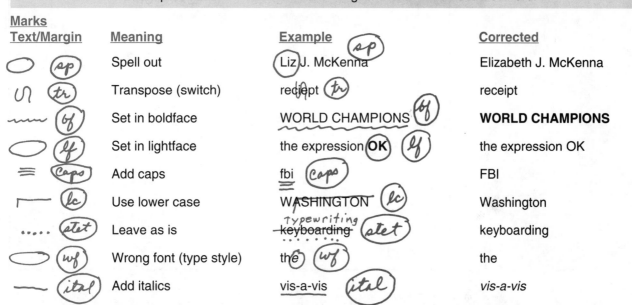

Marks Text/Margin	Meaning	Example	Corrected
⟨⟩ (sp)	Spell out	Liz J. McKenna (sp)	Elizabeth J. McKenna
⟲ (tr)	Transpose (switch)	reciept (tr)	receipt
﹏ (bf)	Set in boldface	WORLD CHAMPIONS (bf)	**WORLD CHAMPIONS**
⟨⟩ (lf)	Set in lightface	the expression **OK** (lf)	the expression OK
≡ (caps)	Add caps	fbi (caps)	FBI
⌐ (lc)	Use lower case	WASHINGTON (lc)	Washington
..... (stet)	Leave as is	typewriting / keyboarding (stet)	keyboarding
⟨⟩ (wf)	Wrong font (type style)	the (wf)	the
—— (ital)	Add italics	vis-a-vis (ital)	vis-a-vis

The following two documents illustrate the use of proofreaders' marks. The first document has been proofread. The second document is the final copy. Study each proofreaders' mark in the first document and note the correction in the finished copy. This process is designed to reinforce your knowledge of proofreaders' marks. You will have many opportunities to apply these marks to business documents as you work through the chapters of the text.

GORDON LOFT & SPENCER

2139 BLAKE ROAD
ATLANTA, GA 34122
706 555-3440
FAX: 706 555-3445

DESIGN CONSULTANTS

November 1, 19XX

Andrea McPherson
    Purchasing Coordinator
Small Business Systems
P.O. Box 445
Elko, NV 89801

Dear Andrea

Thank you for being one of several 100s of people in Reno who visited our booth at the Computer Expo on Oct. 15 and 16. You were also kind enough to complete the product information card. Now I am very interested in knowing whether or not you recieved the follow up proposal I sent on Oct. 20. If you did, can I be of further asssistance to you in your planning? If you did not, please call my office at (706) 555-3440 today for your own personal copy. It will be sent to you by via overnight mail.

Sincerely

Oliver Preston
Design Consultant

wsw

GORDON LOFT & SPENCER

DESIGN CONSULTANTS

2139 BLAKE ROAD
ATLANTA, GA 34122
706 555-3440
FAX: 706 555-3445

November 1, 19XX

NO PUNCTUATION = OPEN punctuation

Andrea McPherson
Purchasing Coordinator
Small Business Systems
P.O. Box 445
Elko, NV 89801

Dear Andrea

Thank you for being one of several hundreds of
people who visited our booth at the Computer Expo in
Reno on October 15 and 16. You also were kind
enough to complete the product information card.

Now I am very interested in knowing if you received
the follow-up proposal I sent on October 20. If you
did, can I be of further assistance to you in your
planning? If you did not, please call my office at
(706) 555-3440 today for your personal copy. It
will be sent to you via overnight mail.

Sincerely

Oliver Preston
Design Consultant

wsw

The following two documents illustrate the use of proofreaders' marks. The first document has been proofread. The second document is the final copy.

Study each proofreaders' mark on the first document, and note the correction in the finished copy. This process will reinforce the application of these proofreaders' marks.

Midwes⊤ ⊤elegraph and Communications

One Center Drive • Chicago, Illinois 56103
312 555-9878 • Fax 312 555-9877

October 10, 19XX

(lc) TELEDYNE EXPORTERS
900 Hartford Blvd.
Farmington, MI 06032

(cap) Ladies and gentlemen:

(bf) ⌐Congratulations!⌐

(lc) On behalf of our President, **Lureen Lombardi**, I wish to *(bf)*
extend ⌐ congratulations on the recognition of your *(lc)*
(lc) firm as The Small Business of the Year for the State *(ital)*
of Michigan. It is an honor well deserved.

(wf) We are especially pleased that you (cited) our cic *(cap)*
For telephone system playing a major role in your
success. A satisfied customer is our best
advertisement.

(stet) Jeanne
~~Jean~~ Kershner, your ƒales ⟋epresentative, will stop in *(lc)* *(lc)*
your office next week to personally express our
appreciation—a limited edition copy of Tomorrows
Technology Today.

Sincerely,

Peter Polari
Executive Assistant

bnn

MidwesT Telegraph and Communications

One Center Drive • Chicago, Illinois 56103
312 555-9878 • Fax 312 555-9877

October 10, 19XX

Teledyne Exporters
900 Hartford Blvd.
Farmington, MI 06032

Ladies and Gentlemen:

Congratulations!

On behalf of our president, Lureen Lombardi, I wish
to extend congratulations on the recognition of your
firm as the *Small Business of the Year* for the state
of Michigan. It is an honor well deserved.

We are especially pleased that you cited our CIC
telephone system for playing a major role in your
success. A satisfied customer is our best
advertisement.

Jean Kershner, your sales representative, will stop
in your office next week to personally express our
appreciation—a limited edition copy of Tomorrow's
Technology Today.

Sincerely,

Peter Polari
Executive Assistant

bnn

PROOFREADING ALERT

Always check all titles—of books, articles, magazines, movies, television shows, etc.—against the original copy.

Let's see how you do when you apply some of the proofreaders' marks you have just learned to a simple document. The following paragraph contains six errors. Refer to your Proofreader's Cue Card, and insert the correct proofreaders' marks.

NOTICE TO ALL Sales PERSONNEL (CAPS)

Begining next monday, January 15, your (CAPS) monthly sales reports will be due on the 15th of each month. When the 15th falls on a week end, reports are due on the following Monday.

The new report forms, designed by your task force, are are now available from Sandi in Corporate Accounting.

Check your work in the Answer Key at the back of this book.

You will have many opportunities to use proofreaders' marks as you work through the chapters of the text.

PERFORMANCE GOALS

UPON COMPLETING THIS UNIT, YOU WILL BE ABLE TO:

● Correct the formats of business letters and memorandums according to widely accepted formatting standards

● Correct the formats of agendas, minutes, and press releases to improve readability

● Use proofreaders' marks to indicate corrections

● Correct common spelling errors to produce acceptable business documents

● Use plurals and possessives correctly

● Use frequently confused words correctly

UNIT
1

PROOFREADING
BASIC
SHORT
DOCUMENTS

It is hard to imagine the volume of business letters that are written annually in the United States. According to the Yankee Group, one study projected that United States businesses stored about 672 billion paper documents in 1993. Perhaps someone should research the number of letters that are actually read, to be followed by a study of how many letters receive positive responses. The resulting figures would be surprisingly low.

Your objective is to produce letters of such superior appearance and accuracy that they are both read and responded to. As you work through this chapter, you have three goals:

- Review business letter formats.
- Improve your skill in spelling and word usage.
- Develop your skill in proofreading.

PROOFREADING FOR FORMAT
STANDARD LETTERS

The focus of this chapter is on proofreading short business letters. As you work through this text, you will note a wide variety of business formats for most document types. Letters, however, conform to one of three styles: block letter format, modified block format, and simplified letter format. When you are proofing a document for format, these questions apply regardless of style or type. Ask yourself:

- Is the document placed attractively on the page? Or is it noticeably too high or too low?
- Do the margins appear to be even?
- Is spacing within the document consistent?
- Are the parts in proper order?
- Are the parts positioned correctly in relation to one another?
- Is the punctuation style consistent with accepted standards?

Sample letters and formatting checkpoints appear on the following pages as a reference to be used when you are scanning the format of business letters for acceptability. Begin your work by reviewing these standard formats.

BLOCK LETTER FORMAT WITH OPEN PUNCTUATION

Ultra Feminique

MALL OF AMERICA
3440 CLIDING DRIVE
BLOOMINGTON, MN 54408
612 555-4566
FAX 612 555-4555

July 27, 19XX

Ms. Jeanette Godwin
5839 Clarita Court
White Plains, NY 10604

Dear Ms. Godwin

Thank you for responding so quickly to our letter regarding the status of your charge account.

We were very happy to learn that you are returning to this area and will once again be shopping at Ultra Feminique. Please accept the enclosed gift certificate as a "Welcome Back" gift from your friends here.

Sincerely

Cassandra Washington
Personal Shopper

ytt

Enc.

PROOFREADING ALERT
Whenever you see opening quotation marks, stop to make sure that there are closing quotation marks.

FORMATTING CHECKPOINTS

✔ Begin all lines at the left margin.
✔ Do not put a colon after the salutation or a comma after the closing when using open punctuation.
✔ Use the print preview feature of your software to position the letter vertically on the page.

MODIFIED BLOCK LETTER FORMAT

eurological Institute

July 1, 19XX

Elaine Sudavi, M.D.
6600 Atwood Lane
Wheaton, IL 60187

Dear Dr. Sudavi:

Enclosed are the three brochures you requested at
the recent meeting of the Illinois Neurological
Specialists.

Our representative, Theodore Cosby, will visit your
office within the next three weeks. He will be
happy to answer any additional questions you may
have.

                    Sincerely,

                    Renee LaFontaine
                    Account Manager

pqr

Enc.

5771 14th Avenue N.W. • Dandylion, CA 99705 • 707-555-9876 • Fax 707-555-9888

FORMATTING
CHECKPOINTS

✔ Begin the date and closing lines at center.
✔ Put a colon after the salutation and a comma after the closing.
✔ Either block or indent the first lines of paragraphs.
✔ Single-space the body of the letter; double-space between
    paragraphs.
✔ Use the print preview feature of your software to position
    the letter vertically.

SIMPLIFIED LETTER FORMAT

Rhode
Island
Yachting
Society

21 Theilen's Bay Rd.
Clonesby
Rhode Island
32114
401-555-0965
Fax 401-555-0999

July 1, 19XX

Robert S. Bruce
8811 Professional Plaza
Barrington, RI   02806

ANNOUNCEMENT OF NEXT RIYS MEETING

The next meeting of the Rhode Island Yachting
Society will be held on Saturday, August 5,
19XX, at the Narragansett Yacht Club, 10 a.m.
to 1 p.m.

As we requested at our May meeting, please
plan to bring 15 copies of your committee's
annual report.

MONTE POPOVILIA, PRESIDENT

bnn

PROOFREADING ALERT

Whenever a specific day and date are mentioned, check a calendar to make sure the day is correct. For example, this letter refers to Saturday, August 5. Check a calendar to make sure that August 5 falls on a Saturday. (You cannot confirm the date in the example shown because the year is not given.)

FORMATTING CHECKPOINTS

✔ Begin all lines at the left margin.
✔ Replace the salutation with an all-caps subject line. Omit the word subject.
✔ Leave a triple space above and below the subject line.
✔ Omit the complimentary closing. Key the writer's name and title in all caps four lines below the last line of the body of the letter.

FORMATTING SPECIAL PARTS OF LETTERS

Electronic Designers Inc.
421 Tyler Road • Cascade, OR 70532
503 555-5848   Fax-503 555-5844

July 1, 19XX

Attention M. J. Juarez
International Technologies
P.O. Box 255
Lewiston, ME 04240

Ladies/Gentlemen:

SUBJECT: SUPER BOWL TV COMMERCIAL

Your television commercial which aired during
halftime of the Super Bowl included one serious
error: The circuitry is an RX-2 design rather than
an RX-12 design (see the enclosed brochure).

We think you should take the necessary steps to
correct this as it could cause serious problems for
communications developers using the system.

Sincerely,

Clarissa LaBeau
Systems Design Consultant

ghf

Enc.

copy K. Yin

PROOFREADING
ALERT

If the item in parentheses is not a complete sentence, check to be sure that the period is positioned outside the closing parenthesis.

FORMATTING
CHECKPOINTS

✔ <u>Attention line</u>. Position as the first line of the inside address.
  Either underline or key in all caps.
✔ <u>Group salutation</u>. Use either *Ladies/Gentlemen* or *Ladies and
  Gentlemen* when writing to a group of people. When all
  addressees have the same status, you may prefer an
  inclusive salutation such as *Dear Manager*.
✔ <u>Subject line</u>. Key the subject line in all caps. The use of the
  word SUBJECT is optional.
✔ <u>Enclosure notation</u>. Key the enclosure notation (*Enclosure* or
  Enc.) a double space below the writer's title.
✔ <u>Copy notation</u>. Key the copy notation (*copy* or *c*) a double
  space below the enclosure notation.

The first step in proofreading is to scan the document for format. Scan—do not read—each of the following four letters. Use the lines at the bottom to list any mistakes you note. Refer to the preceding sample letters as necessary.

17654 George Street
Seattle, WA 98005
206-555-7968
206-555-8898 Fax

August 15, 19XX

Daniel J. Warsaw
425 Marquette, Apt. 2
Nicholasville, KY 40356

Dear Mr. Warsaw

Your order for two dozen Superwrite printer ribbons
was shipped today via Reliable Mail Services.

Your continued support is appreciated.

Sincerely

Lillian Holcomb
Mail Order Supervisor

lls

Letter 1. Is this format correct?   Yes____ No ✗
If not, indicate the incorrect feature.

Too high on page

Check your work in the Answer Key at the back of this book.

QED, Inc

2655 Troutcreek Road
Penn, WI 75220
715-555-0003
715-555-0033 Fax

September 17, 19XX

Superior Temporaries
9090 Belcrest Towers
Hyattsville, MD 20782

TESTING VALIDATION

In agreement with our contract, we have
completed the validation of your testing
materials. While the attached summary will
provide you with details, we are especially
pleased to be able to inform you that your
testing materials are superior in every
respect.

We are looking forward to our meeting next week
to discuss the second phase of this project.

JANET K ARCHER, TESTING SPECIALIST

ceb

Letter 2. Is this format correct?   Yes____ No ✗____
If not, indicate the incorrect feature.

Triple space above/below subject line
two vertical space before signature
Inconsistent spacing

HOUSING AUTHORITY

34 Government Center
Cleveland, OH 31587

216-555-1239   Fax: 216-555-1233

October 31, 19XX

David M. Rockwood III
Rockwood International
PO Box 7755
Cleveland, OH   44114

Dear Mr. Rockwood

    Thank you for your generous contribution
to the Interim Housing Development Project.
The support of persons like yourself makes
the difference between success and failure of
this important project.

    We would like to honor you at a
reception to be held at the Greater Cleveland
Civic Center on Friday, December 10, 19XX, at
seven o'clock. We hope you will be able to
be present.

Cordially

Elizabeth Holmsted
Development Specialist

dlm

Letter 3. Is this format correct?   Yes____ No ☒
If not, indicate the incorrect feature.

Paragraphs should not be indented
more space under date and closing

Check your work in the Answer Key.

Nevada
Small
Business
Association...........................
10075 Circle Avenue
Breathrite, NV 96115
702•555•7689
702•555•7666

November 10, 19XX

Nancy Andersen
Secretaries Plus
4545 Rainbow Avenue
Reno, NV 89509

Dear Nancy

Thank you for the excellent
presentation you made at the Nevada
Small Business Association last week.

The program committee has voted to
pursue some of the goals you
suggested. We are eagerly
anticipating our first meeting.

Thanks again.

Sincerely

Barbara Bushart
Corresponding Secretary

clb

Letter 4. Is this format correct? Yes_____ No _✗_
If not, indicate the incorrect feature.

Margins to big
use default 1"
_____
_____
_____

Check your work in the Answer Key.

Read the business letter illustrated below. Note the highlighted misspelled words. These are just five of the most commonly misspelled words in business correspondence. Are you confident of the correct spelling of each? Look up each word in your dictionary. Were you correct? This section of Chapter 1 will reinforce your spelling skills.

GLOBE ✦ TRAVEL

7221 Sundial Rd, Suite 145   Perimeter, Montana 54936
406/555-7655   Fax-406/555-7778

January 15, 19XX

1. recognize
2. affected
3.
4. february
5. accommodate

Janus Interiors
450 Trinity Avenue
St. Paul, MN 55106

Ladies:

Thank you for submitting your proposal for our design project so promptly. We **recognise** that our tight deadlines might have **effected** your bidding, but we must **procede** as quickly as possible.

Your presentation is scheduled for Monday, **Febuary** 5 at 10:00 a.m. in Room A-1. This room will **accomodate** 20 persons. If you have any questions, please call our project coordinator, Matt Kravus, at Ext. 3300.

Sincerely,

Connie Dearth
Project Supervisor

Proofreading for accuracy of the text is dependent on your ability to recognize errors. Each of the chapters in Units One through Three will reinforce your skill in spotting and correcting errors in language skills.

The spell check feature of word processors has created a false sense of security among users. For example, suppose the following sentence appeared on your screen:

There lack of committment to the corporate goals effected there productivity.

This sentence contains four spelling errors. However, if you did a spell check on this sentence, only *committment* would be highlighted. The two occurrences of *there* and the single occurrence of *effected* would be overlooked because each is spelled correctly but used incorrectly.

It is still imperative that originators of documents and support persons possess strong spelling skills. While most of us do not think of "rules" when spelling, knowing that specific principles of word formation do govern the spelling of many words can be helpful. This section will help you refine your personal spelling ability by reviewing common spelling principles and giving you an opportunity to apply the principles in spelling related words.

◀ **PROOFREADING POINTERS**

- Know your own spelling weaknesses.
- Keep a current list of words you misspell or misuse. You will find that you tend to repeat these. Recognizing them is the first step to improvement.
- Listen to yourself. Pronounce words correctly; enunciate clearly.
- Spell check every document.

One of the difficulties of learning spelling principles is that there often are exceptions. Therefore, as you work through this section, recognize that the principle is *usually* applied. A dictionary, a word book, and a spell checker are absolutely essential tools for everyone who produces business documents. When in doubt about spelling, look up the word either manually or technologically.

A number of spelling principles must be learned to become a proficient speller.

▼ PRINCIPLE 1: The Silent *e*

- Drop the silent *e* when adding a suffix beginning with a vowel.

Base word	Suffix	Correct spelling
receiv<u>e</u>	<u>i</u>ng	receiving
advis<u>e</u>	<u>o</u>ry	advisory

PROOFREADING POINTERS

- When looking up some words, you will find two spellings listed. The first listing is often the preferred spelling and should be used.
- Two common business words fall into this category. Preferred spellings: *acknowledgment* and *judgment.*

- Retain the silent *e* when adding a suffix beginning with a consonant.

Base word	Suffix	Correct spelling
tim<u>e</u>	<u>l</u>y	timely
grat<u>e</u>	<u>f</u>ul	grateful

- Retain the silent *e* when adding a suffix to a word ending in *ee*.

agr<u>ee</u>	<u>i</u>ng	agreeing
fr<u>ee</u>	<u>l</u>y	freely

▼ PRINCIPLE 2: *ie* or *ei?*

Remember the familiar saying: *i* before *e* except after *c* or when sounded like *a* as in *neighbor* or *weigh.*

<u>ie</u>:	friend, pier, believe
<u>ei</u>:	receive, reign, perceive

Common exceptions	height, foreign, leisure

Refer to Principles 1 and 2, and complete the following short exercise. One word of each of the following pairs is spelled correctly. Circle the correctly spelled word in each pair.

1. arrangeing   (arranging)   _____
2. (actively)   activly   _____
3. (appropriately) appropriatly   _____
4. (receivables)   receiveables   _____
5. decieve   (deceive)   _____
6. (lien)   lein   _____
7. (decreeing)   decreing   _____
8. (deleting)   deleteing   _____
9. accrueing   (accruing)   _____
10. (management)   managment   _____

Check your work in the Answer Key. If you circled the incorrect word in any pair, write the correct spelling on the line provided.

▼PRINCIPLE 3: *ie* or *y*?

Consonants or vowels are the key to using the proper ending of a word.

- When a word ends in *y* preceded by a consonant, change the *y* to *i* and add the suffix.

Base word	Correct spelling
beauty	beautiful
inaccuracy	inaccuracies

- When a word ends in *y* preceded by a vowel, do not change the *y* to *i*; add the suffix to the base word.

Base word	Correct spelling
display	displaying
employ	employable

Common exceptions	lay ⇨ laid, pay ⇨ paid, say ⇨ said

- When a word ends in *ie*, change *ie* to *y* before adding *ing*.

Base word	Correct spelling
lie	lying
tie	tying

In the following short exercise, refer to Principle 3 and combine each word and ending to form a new, correctly spelled word. Write the new word on the line at the right.

1.	directory	+ s	=	_directories_
2.	customary	+ ly	=	_customarily_
3.	employ	+ s	=	_employs_ ✓
4.	rely	+ ance	=	
5.	survey	+ ing	=	
6.	library	+ s	=	
7.	opportunity	+ s	=	
8.	policy	+ s	=	
9.	display	+ ing	=	
10.	loyalty	+ s	=	

Check your work in the Answer Key. If you spelled any word incorrectly, draw a single line through it and write the correct spelling above it.

▼ PRINCIPLE 4: Final Consonants

Knowing when to double final consonants is another troublesome spelling principle. The following two guidelines generally apply. Review the exceptions carefully.

- Do not double a final consonant if the suffix begins with a consonant.

Base word	Suffix	Correct spelling
pay	ment	payment
commit	ment	commitment

- When the word has two or more syllables and the accent is on the second syllable, *do* double the final consonant before adding the suffix.

Base word	Suffix	Correct spelling
commit	ed	committed
occur	ence	occurrence
equip	ing	equipping

- There are several exceptions to Principle 4.
  Use your dictionary as necessary; remember to select the first (preferred) spelling. If you or the originator of the document chooses to use the second spelling, be sure to use it consistently throughout the document.

Common exceptions

Base word	Preferred spelling	Acceptable spelling
benefit	benefited	benefitted
cancel	canceled (*but* cancellation)	cancelled
travel	traveling	travelling

One word of each of the following pairs is spelled correctly. Circle the correctly spelled word in each pair. Refer to Principle 4 as often as needed.

1. occurring   occuring   _____
2. controling   controlling   _____
3. creditted   credited   _____
4. efficeincy   efficiency   _____
5. beginning   begining   _____

Check your work in the Answer Key. If you circled any incorrect word, write the correct spelling on the line at the right.

▼PRINCIPLE 5: Troublesome Word Endings

Certain word endings cause spelling difficulties. Three of the more common groupings of these are covered in this section.

• Ible/able. Three tips will help you add the correct ending to these words.

1. *Able* is the more commonly used ending.
2. *Able* is usually added to complete words.
3. *Ible* is usually added to incomplete words.(But *ible* usually follows syllables ending in *ss*: access + ible = accessible.)

Since many frequently used words end in *ible*, you should use your spell checker or your dictionary whenever you are in doubt.

Complete words	depend + able like + able	dependable likeable
Incomplete words	elig + ible leg + ible	eligible legible
Common words	convertible resistible	

• <u>Ceed/cede/sede</u>. Three tips will help you master these.

1. *Cede* is the most frequently used ending.
2. Only three words end in *ceed*: proceed, exceed, and succeed.
3. Only one word ends in *sede*: supersede.

• <u>Ery/ary</u>. Knowing that *ary* is the more common ending will help you. However, note that there is one very common business word ending in *ery: stationery*. A tip for *stationery*: station*er*y is pap*er* used to write a lett*er*.

• <u>Ize/ise/yse</u>. Two tips will simplify these endings for you.

1. There are over ten times as many words ending in *ize* as in *ise*.

criticize   jeopardize   modernize
televise   advise

2. Only one commonly used word ends in *yze*: analyze.

One word in each of the following pairs is spelled correctly. Circle the correctly spelled word in each pair. Refer to Principle 5 as often as needed.

1.	exchangeible	(exchangeable)	_____
2.	(utilize)	utilise	_____
3.	(exceed)	excede	_____
4.	(complimentary)	complimentery	_____
5.	apologise	(apologize)	_____
6.	(respectable)	respectible	_____
7.	(precede)	preceed	_____
8.	recognise	(recognize)	_____
9.	(transferable)	transferible	_____
10.	(dietary)	dietery	_____

Check your work in the Answer Key. If you circled any incorrect word, write the correct spelling on the line at the right.

Check the following paragraphs from business letters for spelling errors. Circle any incorrectly spelled words, and write the correct form on the lines below each paragraph.

1. Thank you for (submiting) your suggestions for (improveing) our instructional program. It was certainly timely as we are just beginning to (activly) seek the ideas of people in the field.

   submitting _____ improving _____
   actively _____ _____

2. In your (judgement) were we correct in (beleiving) that there were too many (inaccuracys) in our recent newsletter? Should we have assumed that a (proficeint) worker would have noticed these?

   judgment _____ believing _____
   inaccuracies _____ proficient _____

Check your work in the Answer Key.

Check the following paragraphs from business letters for spelling errors in word endings. Circle any incorrectly spelled words, and write the correct form on the lines below each paragraph.

1. It certainly was reasonible for you to assume that you were eligable for the promotion. However, I must emphasise that the final choice was based on a combination of basic and supplementery factors, all of which were listed in the advertisement.

   _____ _____
   _____ _____

2. Please note that accounts receiveable does not balance for last month. You also need to itemise all accounts payible when submitting your report. Please procede to do so immediately.

   _____ _____
   _____ _____

Check your work in the Answer Key.

As you develop your skill in knowing what to look for, you also want to improve your ability in knowing how to find it. Each PERFORMANCE CHALLENGE section begins with valuable pointers for improving your proofreading skill. Read each pointer. Do you observe each of these every time you proofread a document?

Proofreading techniques before printing:

1. Run a spell check on every document.
2. View the document in print preview for attractive placement.

Proofreading short documents such as business letters:

1. Scan the document. Is the spacing consistent?
2. Begin proofing at the date line.
3. Proof the lines of the inside address carefully.
4. Is the salutation consistent with the name of the addressee? An attention line does not determine the salutation.
5. Check the signature lines. Are the writer's name and title correct?
6. Is the copy notation correct and complete? You may wish to add the file name to the copy notation (for example, abc/augbill).
7. Is an enclosure notation included if needed?
8. Read the document for content and meaning.
   Ask yourself the following questions:
   • Does each sentence complete a thought?
   • Is each sentence grammatically correct?
   • Are all words used and spelled correctly?

The following document illustrates the use of some of the proofreaders' marks presented in the Introduction. If you have not already done so, remove the Proofreaders' Cue Card from the inside back cover. Use the card as a reference point, and study each mark to see how it has been applied.

DOCUMENT WITH PROOFREADERS' MARKS

**HOLDINGFORD
LIFE INSURANCE**
16 DOWNSVIEW CIRCLE
MONTGOMERY
ALABAMA 11307
PHONE: 205 555 4354
FAX: 205 555 4333

August 11, 19XX

Ms. Danielle Morse-Wong
7602 Archer Avenue
Colorado Springs, CO 80901

Dear Mrs. Morse-Wong

Enclosed is the ʌrenewal certificate for your term life

ss

sp ins. policy #A-776Q. If you have any questions, cap

please call your agent at (314) 555-9090 X235.

Sincerely

Marcus Popovitz
sp Sales Rep.

abb

Enc.

Document 1: You will now have an opportunity to apply proofreaders' marks to a short letter. The following letter needs to be proofread. First, refer to the letter formats on pages 3-7 as you scan the format. Then, using your Proofreaders' Cue Card, apply the proofreader's marks needed to correct the copy. Follow these instructions:

1. Scan the copy for format errors.
2. Proof the copy for spelling errors.
3. Spell out all dates.
4. Add a new paragraph before the sentences beginning "Since we..." and "Please submit..."

modified block letter closed punt.

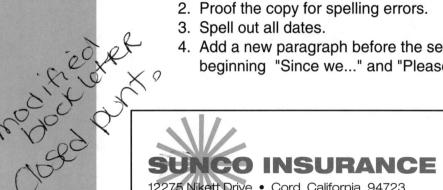

SUNCO INSURANCE

12275 Nikett Drive • Cord, California 94723
209-555-4322 • Fax: 209-555-4333

SP (Dec.) 12, 19XX

Forms Plus, Inc.
P.O. Box 23
Greenwood, IN 46795

Ladies and Gentlemen:

SP This is an official acknowledgement of reciept of
your bid of (Oct.) 31, 19XX, to supply insurance forms
for a period of one year. Since we requested this
bid, our managment has issued a new budget advisery
and this item has been deleted. For that reason,
we are unable to procede with forms design. Please SP
submit a new bid, to supergede this one, on (Jan) 1, SP
19XX. We would be interested in talking further
with you then.

Sincerly

Harry A. Ransom
Director, Client Relations

xxx

Document 2: Scan the following short letter for consistency of format. Remember, a careful business writer uses at least two paragraphs in a letter. Use proofreaders' marks to indicate any corrections.

Simplified

CAP*Link* HEALTH

16 Blenders Way
Athens, GA 30622
706-555-7000
Fax: 706-555-7070

September 30, 19XX

Ana Alicia Guiterrez
1005 Sycamore - Apt. #25
Athens, GA
30615

CONFIRMATION OF APPOINTMENTS

This letter will confirm the two
appointments made during our telephone
conversation of today: October 5, 19XX, and
October 12, 19XX, both at 1:30 p.m.
Please bring your records from Dr. Gupta with you
as these will be very helpful to us. If you need
to change either of these appointments, please
call my office at least 24 hours in advance.

P.T. Barnesky
Scheduling Director

jhk

PROOFREADING ALERT

If a person's name has two initials rather than a first and middle name, make sure that there is no space between the initials. For example, the person who sent this letter does not use a first or middle name. The person's name should appear as P.T. Barnesky.

Document 3: Proofread the following letter for spelling errors. Place your Proofreaders' Cue Card next to the copy. Refer to it as often as necessary as you develop your skill in using proofreaders' marks.

DAY CARE CENTER

5921 SCORPION WAY · UNIVERSITY HILLS, MD 20783 · 410 555-1234/FAX 410 555-9876

October 5, 19XX

George and Betsy Andropolos
787 Williamsburg Drive
University Hills, MD 20783

Dear Mr. and Mrs. Andropolos

You are invited to a very special occasion at The
ABC Daycare Center on Monday evening, October 21,
19XX, at 7:00 p.m. At that time your daughter,
Chadsey, will be recogniged as the "ABC Acheiver
of the Month."

Chadsey exceled in every area during the month of
September. From the begining she has shown
exceptional abilitys, and we beleive this is only
the beginning of her succeeding academically.

She has truely earned the award. We share your
happyness.

Sincerely

Virginia Copperfield
Director

lkl

Document 4: The following document contains errors in format and spelling. Scan the copy for formatting errors; then proofread for accuracy, inserting the correct proofreaders' marks.

COLTMAN PRINTING, INC.
15582 Hagidone N.
McCaldifax, Massachusetts 14462
617 555 3423
Fax: 617 555 3444

January 15, 19XX

Swain & Simpson, P.C.
P.O. Box 88
Nashville, TN 33570

Ladies and Gentlemen:

Thank you for your recent order for 12 reams of
letterhead stationary. This order will be
imprinted with your current logo and new address,
with one change: The FAX number will preceed the
telephone number.

        We recognise the urgency of this order. We
will procede to place a "rush" on the paper stock
and anticipate shiping the order by February 1. We
will ship a temporary supply by Overnight Express
tomorrow.

Sincerely,

Joseph Capiccio
District Sales Manager

wwr

*I*nteroffice memorandums (usually called memos) are the primary form of written communication within an organization. Many business people will tell you they write many more memos than letters. Memos follow all the principles of good business writing, but they are usually brief, more direct, and less formal than business letters.

Memos can also be more important—to the individual writer. Memos that are sent to or read by persons in management and executive positions can influence promotion decisions. Yes, the memos produced in an office are critical communication documents.

As a proofreader of memos, you have three goals for this chapter:

- Review memo formats.
- Improve your skill in forming plurals and possessives.
- Continue developing your proofreading skill.

PROOFREADING FOR FORMAT

MEMOS

Unlike business letters, interoffice memos use a variety of formats. While the traditional memo format is illustrated on page 28, it is important to remember that there are many other formats used.

Memos may be keyed on plain paper or on printed forms. Regardless of format, memos include specific elements.

MEMO ON PLAIN PAPER

```
MEMORANDUM

TO:        Distribution List

FROM:      Sandi Krenzer
           Correspondence Supervisor

DATE:      February 2, 19XX

SUBJECT:   COMPENSATORY TIME


It has come to my attention that there is some
misunderstanding about the accumulation and use of
compensatory time.  I hope that the following
paragraph from the Support Staff Agreement will
clarify this.

   Par. V, 1a:  Compensatory time is accumulated
   only when the employee is requested by the
   supervisor to work more than 7.5 hours per day
   or 37.5 hours in a given week. Compensatory
   time is calculated in .5 hours and may be
   taken upon prior approval from the supervisor.

If you have any questions, please call me.
Together we can resolve the matter.

fgg

Distribution: A. Alvarez
              B. Johnson
              J. Sanchez-Harris
              N. Streff
              L. Thomason
              J. White-Simmons
              W. Zankov
```

PROOFREADING ALERT

Always compare quoted material to original copy. Also, never change anything in quoted material.

FORMATTING CHECKPOINTS

Follow the memo format of your office or organization.

✔ <u>Printed forms</u>. Align the left margin of your text with memo headings.

✔ <u>Plain paper</u>. Key the word MEMORANDUM in all caps about 1 inch from the top of the page.

✔ Key the date in full.

✔ Key individuals' names and departments (if needed) after the TO. When writing to several persons, substitute *Distribution* or *Distribution List* for the names. Do not use courtesy titles such as *Mr.* or *Ms.*

✔ Use an accurate and concise subject line.

✔ Key *Attachment* rather than *Enclosure* near the bottom of the page when you are sending additional materials.

✔ Key the distribution list a double space below the last item. Key the names in alphabetical order.

Refer to the Formatting Checkpoints and scan the following traditional memo format. Use proofreaders' marks to indicate any format errors.

```
Memorandum


TO:       Distribution List

FROM:     Mr. Matthew Reaume

SUBJECT:  Inventory Closing

DATE:     Mar. 16, 19XX   SP


The shipping room will be closed on Thursday and Friday,
April 20 and 21, for inventory.

As you know, participation is optional.  Employees may
work regular hours at supplemental pay rates or may take
vacation time at one-half credit for those two days.

Please complete the attached form and return it to your
supervisor no later than April 1.

ytt
Attachment
Enc.

Distribution:  D. Annabelle
               G. Brokavic
               H. DeAngelo
               P. Frankel
               V. Horowitz
               N. Petruccio
               W. Roberts
               S. Yunez
```

Check your work in the Answer Key at the back of this book.

The memo below illustrates the format of a printed memo form. After reviewing the format, note the highlighted words and phrases. These represent errors in the formation of plurals and possessives. Can you correct each one? This section of Chapter 2 will help you build your confidence in doing so.

MEMO ON PRINTED FORM

MEMORANDUM

To:	Joanna Grimes	**From:**	P. L. Graznik
Dept.:	Human Resources	**Dept.:**	Accounting
Subject:	Pending Case #345-Q-P	**Date:**	September 3, 19XX

Ben Adams notified me today that we need to provide **copys** of the following items for our **attornies** as quickly as possible.

1. **Bill of ladings** Nos. 352-A through 399-A
2. **Joan Butcher and Greta Deegan's** W-2 forms for last year
3. Our **companies'** policy statement regarding compensation for time worked over 50 hours per week
4. **Two month's** travel claims (January and February) for Walt Elliott

Please notify me when these have been sent. Thanks.

kjl

PROOFREADING ALERT

Whenever you see a numbered list, make sure the numbers are consecutive, that none have been dropped or repeated. If the numbers are followed by a period, make sure that each number in the list is followed by a period.

Forming the plural and possessive forms of most words is an easy task. There are, however, other words that cause all of us to pause and ask questions such as: Do I add *s* or *es*? Does the apostrophe fall before the *s* or after the *s*?

This chapter will review the principles of forming plurals and possessives and help you build your confidence in using these forms.

PRINCIPLES AND PRACTICE
PLURALS

Creating plurals in English is achieved by observing several rules.

- Most plurals are formed by simply adding *s* to the singular form of the word.

Singular form	**Plural form**
computer + <u>s</u> =	computers
envelope + <u>s</u> =	envelopes

- When the noun ends in *s, x, z, ch,* or *sh,* add *es.*

Singular form	**Plural form**
los<u>s</u> + <u>es</u> =	losses
ta<u>x</u> + <u>es</u> =	taxes
raz<u>z</u> + <u>es</u> =	razzes
sear<u>ch</u> + <u>es</u> =	searches
da<u>sh</u> + <u>es</u> =	dashes

- The plural of proper nouns is formed in the same way.

Singular name	**Plural name**
Ros<u>s</u> + <u>es</u> =	Rosses
Fo<u>x</u> + <u>es</u> =	Foxes
Swart<u>z</u> + <u>es</u> =	Swartzes
Bir<u>ch</u> + <u>es</u> =	Birches
Mar<u>sh</u> + <u>es</u> =	Marshes

- When the noun ends in *y* preceded by a *vowel,* simply add an *s.*

Singular form	**Plural form**
holid<u>ay</u> + <u>s</u> =	holidays
journ<u>ey</u> + <u>s</u> =	journeys

- When the noun ends in *y* preceded by a *consonant,* change the *y* to *ie* and add *s.*

Singular form	Plural form
indus<u>try</u> + <u>s</u> =	industries
compa<u>ny</u> + <u>s</u> =	companies

- When a noun ends in *fe,* generally change the *fe* to *ve* and add *s.*

Singular form	Plural form
li<u>fe</u> + <u>s</u> =	lives
wi<u>fe</u> + <u>s</u> =	wives

- When the noun ends in *o,* generally add *s.*

Singular form	Plural form
radi<u>o</u> + <u>s</u> =	radios
phot<u>o</u> + <u>s</u> =	photos

> *Common exceptions*

- There are several common nouns ending in *o* that form the plural by adding *es.* Because there is no pattern to these formations, always check the dictionary or word book when you are in doubt.

Singular form	Plural form
her<u>o</u> + <u>es</u> =	heroes
tomat<u>o</u> + <u>es</u> =	tomatoes

- Add the plural to the main word of compound expressions and hyphenated words.

Singular form	Plural form
board of education	boards of education
attorney-at-law	attorneys-at-law

Write the plural form of each of the following words on the line at the right. Refer to the principles for forming plurals. Use your dictionary or spell checker when you are in doubt.

1. monopoly — *monopolies*
2. highways — *highways*
3. business — *businesses*
4. editor-in-chief — *editor-in-chiefs*

5. currency   *currencies*
6. bush   *bushes*
7. bill of lading   *bills of ladings*
8. photocopy   *photocopies*
9. passkey   *passkeys*
10. branch   *branches*

Check your work in the Answer Key. If you misspelled any word, cross it out and write the correct form above it.

PRINCIPLES AND PRACTICE

POSSESSIVES

A possessive noun or pronoun denotes ownership. The possessive form of a noun uses an apostrophe.

▼ **PRINCIPLE 1: Common Formation of Possessives**

The possessive of nouns is formed in one of two ways:

- By adding *'s* to most singular nouns: *employee* becomes *employee's*.

- By adding *'* to most plural nouns: *employees* becomes *employees'*.

The possessive form is used for pronouns showing possession.

Pronoun	Possessive form
I, me	my, mine
you	your, yours
he, him, she, her, it	his, her, hers, its
we, us	our, ours
they, them	their, theirs
who, whom	whose

Write the possessive form of each of the following words on the line at the right. Refer to Principle 1.

Base word	Possessive form
1. champion	*champion's*
2. assistants	*assistants'*
3. manager	*manager's*
4. presidents	*presidents'*

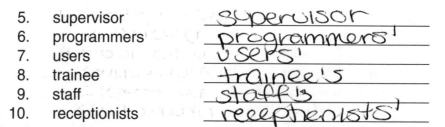

5.	supervisor	supervisor
6.	programmers	programmers'
7.	users	users'
8.	trainee	trainee's
9.	staff	staff's
10.	receptionists	receptionists'

> *Check your work in the Answer Key. If you formed the possessive of any word incorrectly, cross it out and write the correct form above it.*

▼ PRINCIPLE 2: Troublesome Possessives

Spelling a possessive form requires you to consider the following points:

• When two nouns both share ownership, only the second noun is possessive.

> David and Patrick's mother, Diane, is an attorney.
> (the same mother)

• When two nouns have separate ownership, both nouns are possessive.

> Deanna's and John's mothers cochaired the benefit dance. (separate mothers)

• The possessive of some common plural words is always formed by adding 's.
> men's clothing   women's concerns   children's books

• The possessive of units of time follows a simple guideline:

When referring to one unit of time only, add 's.
> one week's pay   one month's notice

When referring to two or more units of time, add s'.
> two weeks' vacation   ten years' seniority

• The possessive form is usually used before a gerund (a verb ending in -ing acting as a noun).

<u>Correct usage</u>	<u>Incorrect usage</u>
my responding	*me* responding
your coming	*you* coming

exceptions

men's
women's
children's

5-5c

5-5c

5-5A

5-5f

5-5e
5-7e

Gerund ends in ING

Authorities differ on the formation of the possessive with inanimate nouns (the names of things rather than people or animals, such as *table* versus *child*). Some recommend that the possessive of inanimate objects always be formed by using the word *of*. Other authorities do not agree with this. If the possessive form using ' or 's sounds awkward, use an *of* expression.

Recommended form	Alternate form
leg of the table	table's leg
windows of the building	building's windows

There are some common possessive expressions that are widely used.

a moment's notice	a stone's throw
for heaven's sake	her heart's content

Study each of the following pairs. On the line at the right indicate the correct possessive form by writing A or B. Refer to the principles as needed.

A	**B**	
1. children's center	childrens' center	A
2. three week's vacation	three weeks' vacation	A
3. Jo's and Bob's W-2 forms	Jo and Bob's W-2 forms	B
4. one day's travel pay	one days' travel pay	A
5. Amy's and Marti's skills	Amy and Marti's skills	B A
6. four customers' accounts	four customer's accounts	A B
7. Frank and Ray's store	Frank's and Ray's store	A
8. this weeks' total	this week's total	B A
9. Scott and Sue's child	Scott's and Sue's child	A
10. I oppose their coming.	I oppose them coming.	A

Check your work in the Answer Key. If you selected the incorrect form, study the correct form. If you are having difficulty, review the principles presented in this section.

MASTERY CHECKPOINT ONE

Review the following paragraphs from a memo for the correct use of plurals. Use proofreaders' marks to correct any errors you find.

PROOFREADING ALERT

Words containing repeated vowels (administrative, facility, management) should be proofread carefully. Often the second or third occurrence of the vowel is omitted, resulting in a misspelling.

> The faculty from our three facilitys will meet in the Erickson Administration Building on Friday morning at 10 a.m. The topic will be "Making Media Work for You."
>
> J. G. Francis of Future Look Laboratorys will demonstrate the latest equipment for educational studios: radios, stereos, cameras, and computer presentations.
>
> Dr. Francis will also present the results of several studys that support the importance of visual aids in the classroom.

Check your work in the Answer Key.

MASTERY CHECKPOINT TWO

Review the following paragraphs from a memo for the correct application of the possessive forms. Insert proofreaders' marks to correct the copy.

PROOFREADING ALERT

If a proper name is mentioned more than once, confirm that it is correct each time.

> We have just received an employment application from Katarina Bortsch, a graduate of Milwaukees most prestigious business college. Her skills are excellent, and she can start in just two weeks time. I am considering her for the administrative assistant position in Margaret Bush and David Ray's office.
>
> During her interview, Katarina indicated that she had developed an interest in our company from her mothers close friend who worked for us in the 1970s. Both Katarina's academic and personal background suggest that she would make an excellent employee.
>
> Its been a long time since I have been this impressed with a candidate. I see the possibility of Katarina's being with us for many years to come.

Check your work in the Answer Key.

You have already discovered that proofreading is a composite skill. It requires you to use all of the skills and knowledge you have in both formatting and using correct language to do the best job.

Proofreading is also a cumulative skill. Thus, you will find it helpful to review the techniques you learned in Chapter 1 before you add to your skill by studying the techniques listed here.

When proofreading short documents such as memos, observe the following items:

1. Scan the document.
   - Is the format consistent?
   - Does it conform to an existing in-house format?
2. Proof each line of the heading.
   - Are names and dates correct?
   - Is the subject line accurate?
3. Check pairs of punctuation (quotation marks, parentheses) to be sure the closing one is not omitted.
4. Check the distribution list, if used.
   - Are the names in alphabetic order?
   - If your office uses a ranking order, are the rankings correct?
5. Read each document for accurate content.
   - Does each sentence complete a thought?
   - Is each sentence grammatically correct?
   - Are all words used and spelled correctly?

Document 1: Scan the following memo for correct format. Use your Proofreader's Cue Card as a reference, and apply the proofreaders' marks needed to correct the copy.

MEMORANDUM

TO: Distribution List   DATE: (Jan.) 15, 19XX

FROM: Todd Martinez   SUBJECT: ERROR

(LC) Please refer to page 15 of the Regional Quarterly
Goals (D)istributed at our meeting last Friday and
make the following correction:

    Quarterly Goals for Western Region: 2.5%
    increase

Also enclosed is the third quarter chart I
mentioned.

dsa

Attachment
~~Enclosure~~

Distribution ~~List~~: George Wendt
                        Jane Bryant
                        Traci Cox
                        Brett O'Hanaghan
                        Sally Pilarski
                        Ivan Pretenko
                        James Runciman
                        Heidi Stein

Document 2: Review the following memo for consistency of format. Use proofreaders' marks to indicate any errors.

MEMORANDUM

TO: Luther Kirkendall

FROM: Christine Gwartney

SP   SUBJECT: MAINTENANCE PERFORMANCE

DATE: Feb. 28, 19XX

On Tuesday, February 25, I hosted a group of local bank presidents in our main conference room for a preliminary planning meeting for our United Way campaign. This meeting had been scheduled since November 15 of last year. My room request form (copy attached) requested the following items: six 4-foot tables arranged in a U, an overhead projector and screen, and a podium.

When I arrived for the meeting, I found six rows of tables arranged classroom style, no projector or screen, and no podium. Remnants of the previous night's meeting (coffee cups, markers, etc.) were scattered throughout the room. Fortunately, I had arrived early and immediately called Gene Cisko, the maintenance supervisor. By the time the group arrived, the room was presentable.

Gene indicated that my telephone call was the first time he was aware of the meeting. Would you please look into this matter and meet with me at 2 p.m. on March 2 in my office to discuss it.

pto
Attachment
Enclosure

PROOFREADING ALERT
When two numbers appear together (such as "six 4-foot tables"), spell out one of the numbers to enhance readability.

Document 3: Proofread the following memo for errors in plurals and possessives. Use proofreaders' marks to indicate errors.

```
MEMORANDUM


TO:        G.W. Stockton

FROM:      Frances McInerney

DATE:      March 30, 19XX

SUBJECT:   CLOSING ON 3535 WALTON PLACE


The closing on this property is scheduled as follows:

        April 14, 19XX, at 10:30 a.m.
        Barnes and Noble's law office

In response to your earlier question, its imperative
that both parties be present.  Idaho law requires that
the seller and buyer's signatures be recorded in the
presence of the notary public.

You need to plan on two week's time to receive the deed
from the county clerk.  I would appreciate your calling
me when this document has been recorded.

der
```

Document 4: The last Performance Challenge document in each chapter is cumulative; that is, errors may include all topics covered to that point. As you work your way through this type of document, your confidence in your proofreading ability will grow.

MEMORANDUM

TO: Distribution List
FROM: Joseph Unitas
DATE: December 2, 19XX
SUBJECT: HOLIDAY BENEFIT PARTY

Its holiday time! As we have done for the past seven years, our holiday partys on December 20 and 22, 19XX, will benifit the Salvation Army.

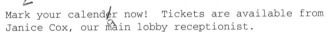

We have arranged a beautiful setting for this years special events--Aspen Lodge at the foot of Snowbird Mountain. The evenings begin at 6:30 p.m.; dinner will be served at 8 p.m. Tickets are $25 each, with half of the procedes from each ticket going directly to the Salvation Army's local projects. Once again several local merchants have donated beautiful gifts as door prizes.

Mark your calender now! Tickets are available from Janice Cox, our main lobby receptionist.

hjk

CHAPTER

3

**PROOFREADING
AGENDAS,
MINUTES, AND
NEWS
RELEASES**

Although letters and interoffice memorandums represent the largest categories of short business documents, there are many other short documents produced in today's businesses. Three of these have been selected to conclude this unit: agendas, minutes, and news (or press) releases.

Here are your goals for this chapter:

- Review guidelines for preparing selected short documents.
- Sharpen your skill in using frequently confused words.
- Further develop your proofreading ability.

PROOFREADING FOR FORMAT

AGENDAS, MINUTES, AND NEWS RELEASES

The formats of the documents selected for this chapter vary from one organization to another. Thus, this section includes some common checkpoints and formats that are applicable in most settings. If formal agendas or minutes are required, you should consult a parliamentary procedure reference source.

INFORMAL AGENDA

```
                MEETING OF THE EMPLOYEE BENEFITS COMMITTEE
                          Jackson International
                             May 15, 19XX

                                AGENDA

        1.  Call to order:  1:00 p.m.

        2.  Approval of minutes from April 15 meeting

        3.  Old business:

            a.  Review of previous year's summary
            b.  Interim report of salary task force
            c.  Follow-up study:  Retirement benefits

        4.  New business:

            a.  Presentation by Health Care Maintenance
                representative
            b.  Preliminary plans for employee
                negotiations
            c.  Other

        5.  Adjournment:  3:30 p.m.
```

FORMATTING CHECKPOINTS

✔ Include the name of the group and the date of the meeting in the heading.

✔ List the meeting topics in order of discussion. Do not add a period at the end of items.

✔ List the topics in the order shown in the sample agenda.

✔ Consult a guide to parliamentary procedure for more formal agendas.

INFORMAL MINUTES OF A MEETING

```
               MEETING OF THE EMPLOYEE BENEFITS COMMITTEE

                           May 15, 19XX

                              MINUTES

CALL TO          The monthly meeting of the Employee Benefits
ORDER            Committee was held on May 15, 19XX, in the Rogers
                 Conference Room.  All members were present.
                 Ruthann Jordan, Health Care Maintenance
                 representative, was also present.

APPROVAL OF      Minutes of the April 15 meeting were approved.
MINUTES

REVIEW OF 19XX   Harry Nogales presented the final draft of the 19XX
SUMMARY          summary.  It was reviewed and approved by the
                 committee.

SALARY TASK      Cassie Douglas, task force leader, presented an
FORCE--INTERIM   interim report on the progress of the Salary Task
REPORT           Force.  She will present a final report at the next
                 meeting.

RETIREMENT       Norton McCloskey reported that retiree benefits had
BENEFITS         risen 3 percent during the past year, FOLLOW-UP
                 consistent with the budget projection.

HEALTH CARE      Ruthann Jordan, area vice president with HCM,
MAINTENANCE      presented her findings of the actual costs of health
                 care at Jackson International.  She then made a
                 formal proposal for a possible agreement between
                 Jackson and HCM.  The committee will study the
                 proposal and respond at the next meeting.

EMPLOYEE         Richard Buzo, chief negotiator, presented a
NEGOTIATIONS     preliminary time table for beginning negotiations
                 with the three employee groups. The committee voted
                 to accept the schedule.

RESOLUTION--     The committee unanimously adopted the following
25-YEAR          resolution to be presented to all employees having
EMPLOYEES        25 or more years of service: WHEREAS, Jackson
                 International recognizes that the contributions of
                 long-term employees play a major role in the
                 continuing success of the corporation, it is
                 RESOLVED that all employees having 25 or more years
                 of service are immediately eligible for five weeks'
                 vacation yearly.

ADJOURNMENT      The meeting was adjourned at 3:25 p.m.
```

FORMATTING CHECKPOINTS

✔ Include the name of the group and the date of the meeting in the heading.

✔ Use side headings to assist the reader in locating information quickly.

✔ List the items in the same order as they appear on the agenda.

✔ Key RESOLVED (or its equivalent) in all caps, when it is used.

✔ Consult a guide to parliamentary procedure for minutes of formal meetings since these are legal documents.

NEWS RELEASE

```
N E W S   R E L E A S E
                        From Demetrius Johns
                        Kansas Business Institute
                        350 First Avenue
                        Atchison, KS  66002
                        (913) 555-3450

                        Release August 15, 19XX

            KBI BOARD APPOINTS NEW PRESIDENT

    ATCHISON, August 10--The Board of Directors

of Kansas Business Institute announces the

appointment of Marianna Coulter as president,

effective October 1, 19XX.

    Dr. Coulter is presently chancellor of

Nebraska Training Centers in Omaha.  She brings a

varied and successful career as an educational

administrator to KBI.

    Dr. Coulter earned her bachelor's and

master's degrees from Oklahoma State University and

her doctorate from Baylor University.  She is a

lifelong resident of the Midwest.
```

PROOFREADING ALERT

Words such as board (of directors), committee, group, jury, etc., are singular collective nouns and usually take the singular form of the verb. Other references to the collective noun in sentences that follow must also be singular. Thus, "the Board (singular) ... announces" (singular) is correct.

FORMATTING CHECKPOINTS

✔ Place identifying information at the top: name, address, and phone number of contact person; and release date.
✔ Begin with an indented date line including the city of the release.
✔ Double-space the body of the release.

Refer to the Formatting Checkpoints for agendas on page 44 and scan the following informal agenda format. Use proofreaders' marks to indicate format errors.

Agenda

```
        MEETING OF THE BUILDING DESIGN COMMITTEE
                      Software 4U
                     June 7, 19XX

                        Agenda

1.  Call to order:  1:30 p.m.

2.  Approval of minutes from May meeting

3.  Old business

    a.  Final action on designs 2 and 3
    b.  Interim action on design 4
    c.  Action on proposal by Landscape
Architects and Industrial Designers

4.  New business:

    a.  Planning for architectural design
    b.          Formation of subcommittee

5.  Adjournment:  3:30 p.m.
```

wrong line look like p.44

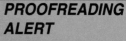

PROOFREADING ALERT

Terms such as *design 1* must be consistent throughout the document. For example: if using *design 1*, then *design 2* should not be *design #2*, or *Design 2*, or *design II*.

Check your work in the Answer Key at the back of this book.

The following paragraph was extracted from the first draft of a committee report. Note the highlighted words. They represent errors in the use of frequently confused words. Can you correct each one? This section of Chapter 3 will help you build confidence in selecting the right word.

```
                                        FIRST DRAFT
                                          6/10/XX


            The Office Support Staff Study

       Committee, consisting of both administrative
   assistance   corre
       assistance and correspondent secretaries, met

       for it's initial meeting on June 9, 19XX.

            Upon the advise of Matt Fisher, the

       committee agreed to except the recommendations

       of the previous committee as a starting point

       for its work.  The ultimate affect of this

       decision should be less delays at latter dates

       when the work load increases.
```

PROOFREADING FOR FORMAT
FREQUENTLY MISUSED WORDS

Certain words are similar in spelling and/or pronunciation, and, as a result, are easily confused and misused. Twenty-five of the more common groupings are listed below to help you further refine your spelling skills.

> • When deciding between similar words, you will need to use a dictionary rather than a word book. Look up the word; read the definition and example carefully; then decide which form is correct.

◀ **PROOFREADING POINTER**

WORD	DEFINITION	EXAMPLE
accept	to receive or agree	I *accept* your explanation
except	excluding; other than	Everyone *except* Lillian attended.
advice	guidance; opinion	His career *advice* was sound.
advise	to give guidance to; to give an opinion	Would you *advise* us to continue?
affect	(v.) to influence	How will the policy *affect* our sales?
effect	(n.) a result	The net *effect* will be minimal.
	(v.) to bring about	Let's *effect* the change immediately.
all ready	fully prepared	We are *all ready* for the show.
already	by now	It is *already* lunch time.
all right	satisfactory; satisfactorily	It seems to be working *all right*.
alright	(a misspelling)	
among	used to compare more than two persons or things	She is *among* the applicants.
between	used to compare two persons or things	The choice is *between* Ann and Ryan.

WORD	DEFINITION	EXAMPLE
assistance	aid; help	Her *assistance* is invaluable.
assistants	helpers	My two *assistants* are very capable.
beside	by the side of	His desk was *beside* mine.
besides	in addition to	*Besides* yourself, who will attend?
capital	wealth; city serving as the seat of government	He raised the *capital* quickly.
capitol	a building for the legislature	Call the lobbyist at the *capitol.*
cite	to refer to	How many references did you *cite?*
site	a location	The plant *site* is centrally located.
sight	vision	I only caught *sight* of the visitor.
complement	to complete	Keyboard accuracy *complements* speed.
compliment	to praise	Your *compliment* was accepted.
council	a group of people	The president's *council* met today.
counsel	to advise	How would you *counsel* the employee?
correspondence	written communication	*Correspondence* should be error-free.
correspondents	people who write	The foreign *correspondents* returned.
device	a tool	She invented the clever *device.*
devise	to invent; to think up	Let's *devise* a solution.
farther	more distant	Is Reno or Fresno *farther* west?
further	additional	The plan has *further* complications.

WORD	DEFINITION	EXAMPLE
fewer	used to refer to countable units	We have *fewer* employees this year.
less	used to refer to quantity or degree	Our employees earned *less* this year.
later	more recent	She was hired at a *later* date.
latter	the second of two	The *latter* option is my choice.
lay	to place	*Lay* the book on the desk.
lie	to rest or recline	The book *lies* on the credenza.
lose	to misplace	Never *lose* your sense of self worth.
loose	not tight	The computer connection was *loose*.
may be	(a verb phrase)	You *may be* right!
maybe	perhaps	*Maybe* we will surpass our goal.
passed	past tense of *pass*	The fiscal year *passed* quickly.
past	that which has already occurred	Our *past* speaks for itself.
principal	chief or main; head of a school; amount of money	The *principal* concern was finances.
principle	a basic rule	Don't compromise your *principles*.
quiet	little or no noise	The conference room was very *quiet*.
quit	to stop doing something	Jon *quit* abruptly.
quite	very; exactly	The business plan is *quite* rigorous.
stationary	not movable	The new desk will be *stationary*.
stationery	writing paper	Please order new *stationery*.
than	compared to	Fran sold more *than* Rex last month.
then	at that time	Can we plan to meet *then*?

Look at the use of the italicized word in each of the following sentences. If the word is used incorrectly, draw a line through it and write the correct word to the left. Refer to the preceding definitions and examples as needed.

1. Any decision you make will be *alright* with me. *all right*
2. When you *lose* a potentially large sale, don't give up.
3. Perhaps *laying* down for a few moments will help you feel better. *lieing*
4. Our inventory has *less* units than a year ago.
5. I inadvertently *past* him a copy of the confidential report. *passed*
6. The trainees discussed classic management *principles*.
7. When will the new *stationary* be ready?
8. Her decision *effected* all of us.
9. The architecture of the *capitol* is very impressive.
10. The city *council* will vote on the issue next week.
11. She's *quiet* a salesperson! *quite*
12. Terri is more competent *then* Gary.
13. Fresh plants will *compliment* the natural decor.
14. I simply cannot *accept* your rationale.
15. The fax machine is a time-saving *devise*. *device*
16. The disgruntled employee *cited* three sections of the contract.
17. Her *advise* was certainly timely. *advice*
18. Beverly has *already* been promoted three times.
19. This matter must be kept *between* the three of us.
20. Her new *assistants* provide her with valuable *assistance*.
21. Please locate the telephone jack *besides* the desk.
22. The quality of her written *correspondence* is excellent.
23. I will proceed no *farther* with the plan.
24. Of the two, my preference is the *later*. *latter*
25. She *maybe* too late in filing her application. *may be*

Review the following short letter for the correct usage of frequently confused words. Use the appropriate proofreaders' marks to indicate any errors.

PERSONNEL ASSISTANTS • *700 Park Avenue* • *Des Moines, Iowa* • *51102*
• *(515) 555-2323* • *Fax (515) 555-2333* •

June 10, 19XX

Hans J. Andreisen
Dataquest Resources
P.O. Box 3354
Jamaica, NY 11432

Dear Dr. Andreisen

Thank you for the excellent advise you provided in
your correspondents of last month.

We have all ready implemented several of your ideas
and find that they are widely excepted by our
employees. In fact, we have had fewer then three
complaints as a result of the changes. While it
maybe too early to draw conclusions, we can say we
are further along in this process then we had
anticipated we would be.

The principals of teamwork that your two assistance
suggested were put into affect immediately. They
have served as effective devises for launching our
new approach to participatory management.

We are ready to proceed to the next phase, which can
only compliment our initial efforts. Thanks again
for your counsel.

Sincerely

Jeanne Marcus
Employee Development Specialist

tty

Check your solution in the Answer Key.

After completing Chapters 1 and 2, you are well on your way to achieving a mastery of proofreading short documents. While the documents covered in this chapter are quite different from those you have worked with so far, there are some additional proofreading techniques you can apply.

When proofreading short documents such as agendas you should check the following items:

1. Scan the document. Are the format and spacing consistent?
2. Are the name of the group and the date of the meeting correct?
3. Do numbers align?
4. Is text aligned with text?
5. Are the items in the order in which they will be discussed in the meeting? Check this with the originator of the agenda or refer to agendas from previous meetings if you are not certain.

Document 1: This section will give you an opportunity to proofread an agenda. Begin by reviewing the formatting checkpoints for agendas on page 44. Use proofreaders' marks to indicate any format errors.

```
                          AGENDA
          MEETING OF THE BUILDING DESIGN COMMITTEE
                       Software 4U
                       May 5, 19XX


          1.  Call to order   2:00 p.m.

          2.  Approval of minutes from Mar. meeting

          3.  Old business:

          a.  Final action on design #1A
          b.  Interim action on designs 2 and 3
          c.  Consideration of design 4

          4.  New business:

              a.  Proposal by Landscape Architects
              b.  Presentation of time chart

          5.  Adjournment:  3 p.m.
```

Document 2: Refer to the agenda you proofread on page 47. The following minutes were prepared after that meeting and are to be proofread. Refer to page 45 to review Formatting Checkpoints for minutes, as necessary. Use proofreaders' marks to indicate any inconsistencies in format.

```
                     MEETING OF THE DESIGN COMMITTEE
                             June 7, 19XX
                               Minutes

     CALL TO ORDER    The monthly meeting of the Building
                      Design Committee was held on June
                      7, 19XX. All members were present.

     APPROVAL OF      Minutes of the May 5 meeting were
     MINUTES          approved.

     Old Business     Interim action on design 4 was
                      tabled until the July meeting.

                      It was resolved that designs 2 and
                      3 did not meet the criteria
                      established and, therefore, are
                      removed from further consideration.

                      A new proposal was presented by
                      Landscape Architects.  The proposal
                      will be studied and reported on at
                      the July meeting.

     NEW BUSINESS   It was recommended that final
     planning for the architectural design begin
     immediately with an ending target date of March
     15, 19XX.

                      A subcommittee (J. Harris,
                      B. Lazarus, W. Gutenberg) was
                      formed to begin work.

     ADJOURNMENT      The meeting adjourned at 3:35 p.m.
```

Document 3: Proofread the following news release for errors in the use of frequently confused words. Use proofreaders' marks to indicate errors.

```
N E W S   R E L E A S E      From Lili Demetrius
                             Bureau of Land Management
                             909 Yukon Way
                             Juneau, AK  99701

                             Release May 1, 19XX

              ENVIRONMENTAL AGENCY ESTABLISHED

     JUNEAU, June 28--The Bureau of Land Management

announces the establishment of the Alaskan Land

Environmental Agency, affective September 1.  The

office of the agency will be located in the

capital in Room 203.

     The work of the new agency will compliment the

environmental studies all ready being done by the

BLM. With the purchase of new measuring devises,

the new agency will require less employees.

     Jake Milligan has been appointed principle

researcher; he will work with three assistance.
```

Documents 4 and 5: You will need to use all of the skills you have acquired in this unit to proofread the following two documents. Scan the documents for format consistency first. Then read the documents for errors in spelling, the formation of plurals and possessives, and the misuse of frequently confused words.

FOREMAN, OGILVY and JAMES, P.C.

607 Bellevue Highway   Phone: 206-333-3440
Seattle, Washington 98339   Fax: 206-333-3443

May 14, 19XX

Perfect Legal Forms
P.O. Box 8900
Darlington, PA   16115

ORDER #682-A

Ladies/Gentleman:

        Upon recieving our resent order #682-A for
Washington Living Will forms (your shiping date of
May 8, 19XX), we were very dissappointed in the
quality of the stationary on which these forms are
printed. These will not feed smoothly through our
lazer printer. With just three day's usage, we have
already used more then 100 sheets to print less then
20 forms.

We have ordered a similiar form from you in the
passed and have always been very satisfied. We are
paticularly disturbed because the catalog discription
states that these are satisfactory for use with all
printers and copiers.

Please except the shipment of these in a seperate
mailing. Also, credit our account and enter a
calcelation for the remainder of our currant order.

Sincerely

Marissa Salvatore
Office Manager

nnm

Document 4

```
MEMORANDUM


TO:  Juliann Lentz
FROM:  Martin Samms
DATE:  Oct. 3, 19XX
SUBJECT:  Employee Benefits


Please inform the employes in your department
that the following changes in benifits will be in
affect as of November 1, 19XX.  If any employees
have not reported change of name, address, or
dependants, they should do so immediately.

Benefit              Change

Daycare assistants   A new provision.  Employees
                     with more then two year's
                     seniority will be eligible
                     up to $50 per month to
                     offset the cost of daycare.
                     Employees should submit
                     their childrens' names and
                     ages to their superviser
                     immediately.

Vision               Increase in inital exam
                     fees from $50 to $60.
                     Corrective lenses for
                     identified site problems
                     will be available every 24
                     months.

ghf
```

Document 5

PERFORMANCE GOALS

UPON COMPLETING THIS UNIT, YOU WILL BE ABLE TO:

- Correct the formats of business reports with citations according to widely accepted formatting standards

- Use proofreaders' marks to indicate corrections

- Proofread copy for agreement of subject and verb, as well as agreement of pronoun and antecedent

- Proofread copy for correct usage of adjectives and verbs

UNIT

11

PROOFREADING

LONG

**BUSINESS
DOCUMENTS**

Business reports are typically multiple-page documents written for a specific purpose. Some common report purposes are to transmit information, to make a proposal, to report on a project or activities, or to introduce and analyze a specific problem. A business report is a detailed communication, which may include facts, proposals, ideas, and graphics. Reports are prepared for both in-house and outside distribution. Reports require very careful preparation and are often desktop published in-house or printed professionally.

In addition to the basic business report, two types of short business reports are produced frequently in the business office:

- An executive summary or abstract, which is a description and summary of a related longer report. Significant data are summarized, but detailed data are not given. The summary usually precedes or is the first section of the complete report.
- A memo report, which is an informal report in memo format usually intended for inside distribution.

Reports may be either formal or informal. Formats vary widely among authorities and businesses; for that reason, no one format should be considered a standard.

Here are your goals for this chapter:

- Review suggested report formats.
- Improve your skill in applying principles of subject-verb agreement.
- Further develop your proofreading skill.

PROOFREADING FOR FORMAT
BUSINESS REPORTS

As stated previously, there is no one standard report format. However, there are guidelines for business reports that can enhance their readability. The following pages will introduce you to the formats of three types of reports:

- An executive summary or abstract
- A memo report
- The body of a short business report

EXECUTIVE SUMMARY

Executive Summary

    The adult learner is a topic of growing interest among educators and business trainers. It is widely recognized that the same techniques and approaches that work in the traditional learning environment usually do not work with the adult learner. Some of the questions our Corporate Training Division addressed were:

* What are the unique characteristics of the adult learner?
* Does our CTD have the resources to train adults effectively?
* In what areas have we been most effective?
* In what areas have we been most ineffective?
* Should training be on an in-house or contract basis?

    To answer these questions, we must analyze the data that is available to us from past training efforts. Before we launch further training programs, we need to complete a detailed needs assessment.

    The training divisions of corporations are growing at unprecedented rates. Training is conducted on a spectrum from basic skills to strategic planning. The Federal government is willing to underwrite some specific training programs. We need a strategic plan to take advantage of these opportunities.

    Recommendation: Develop a training coordinator position within the HR Division, to be filled no later than March 1, 19XX, to develop a comprehensive training plan.

PROOFREADING ALERT

A bulleted list is a list in which each item is preceded by a dot or some other symbol. Make sure that the same symbol is used for each bulleted list in a document.

FORMATTING CHECKPOINTS

✔ Use default margins of 1 inch.
✔ Single-space the summary; double-space between paragraphs.
✔ Use lists rather than narrative whenever possible.
✔ Generally use a serif font, no smaller than 10 points.
✔ Generally do not justify the right margin.
✔ If you use right justification, turn on the hyphenation feature of your software.

MEMO REPORT

TO: Bonita Legeros
FROM: Sharon Hill
DATE: June 10, 19XX
SUBJECT: MEMORANDUM REPORT PREPARATION

This is a sample of a very popular report form, the memo report. Rather than prepare both a report and an accompanying letter or memo, the two are combined. This format is usually used for reports that are fairly short, fewer than three pages.

Subheadings are used throughout the report as shown below.

Summary. The findings of the survey of advertising at Old London Square Mall are similar to the national trends. All the mall stores use, in addition to local cooperative advertising, some type of outside media. The choice of outside media compares quite closely with national trends, since newspapers are listed as most effective and used most frequently, followed by radio, television, direct mailing, and magazines.

Background. Our organization entered into an agreement three months ago with the merchants of the Old London Square Mall to investigate avenues of approach to effective advertising. We assigned methods currently in use throughout the nation, and especially those methods used by businesses in some type of physical-location arrangement (shopping centers, malls, and so on). After gathering the evidence used throughout the country, we prepared a questionnaire and administered it to all the merchants in the Old London Square Mall. The results of both the nationwide survey and the mall survey were then compared.

Findings. Nationwide, merchants agree that individual firms must do more advertising. Cooperative efforts seem to be quite effective when the entire mall conducts some type of sale, but for the rest of the time individual firms must generate sales by individual advertising efforts. The Old London Square Mall merchants agree with this 100 percent. The national use of various types of advertising media differs slightly from what the mall merchants now use.

PROOFREADING ALERT

Similar headings should be formatted consistently throughout the document. Main headings usually appear in all caps and may be boldfaced. Subheadings may use initial caps and be underscored or may be italicized, as shown in this report.

FORMATTING CHECKPOINTS

✔ Use default 1-inch margins.

✔ Single-space the body of the report; double-space between paragraphs. Triple-space before the first line of the body on any page.

✔ Observe the informal memo report format illustrated here.

✔ Use a serif font no smaller than 10 points.

✔ Do not justify the right margin.

CONTINUING PAGE OF MEMO REPORT

```
Bonita Legeros
Page 2
June 10, 19XX

                    Types of Advertising Media*

         Nationwide        Old London Square Mall

         Newspaper         Newspaper
         Television        Radio
         Radio             Television
         Direct mail       Direct mail
         Magazines         Magazines

           *Ranked according to frequency of use

Conclusion.  The use of advertising media by merchants at
the Old London Square Mall closely follows what is being
done on a national scale.  The only difference was in the
ranking of television and radio.  Television is second in
popularity nationwide, and radio is third.  At this mall
radio is second, and television is third.

Recommendations.  Our agreement called for both a written
report and an oral presentation of the findings.  This
information was given to the merchants at their last
monthly meeting.  A recommendation was made that the
merchants use television more than radio in the future.  It
was decided to follow this recommendation for the next six
months, after which a follow-up report will be prepared.

Follow-Up.  Jim Lane will be in charge of the follow-up
research project.  Alice Barnes, June Folton, Bob
```

FORMATTING CHECKPOINTS

✔ If the memo report is more than one page, use a standard second-page heading.

✔ Keep related information such as tables and lists on the same page.

✔ Use the block protect feature of your software to keep blocks of text such as lists or tables on the same page.

BODY OF BUSINESS REPORT

```
                ADVERTISING AT OLD LONDON SQUARE MALL

                  National and Mall Survey Results
```

Summary. The findings of the survey of
advertising at Old London Square Mall are similar
to the national trends. All the mall stores use,
in addition to local cooperative advertising, some
type of outside media. The choice of outside
media compares quite closely with national trends,
since newspapers are listed as most effective and
used most frequently, followed by radio,
television, direct mailing, and magazines.

Background. Our organization entered into an
agreement three months ago with the merchants of
the Old London Square Mall to investigate avenues
of approach to effective advertising. We assigned
methods currently in use throughout the nation,
and especially those methods used by businesses in
some type of physical-location arrangement
(shopping centers, malls, and so on). After
gathering the evidence used throughout the
country, we prepared a questionnaire and
administered it to all the merchants in the Old
London Square Mall. The results of both the
nationwide survey and the mall survey were then
compared.

Findings. Nationwide, merchants agree that
individual firms must do more advertising.
Cooperative efforts seem to be quite effective
when the entire mall conducts some type of sale,
but for the rest of the time individual firms must
generate sales by individual advertising efforts.

FORMATTING CHECKPOINTS

✔ The body of a business report is generally similar to that of a memo report. All other formatting guidelines (margins, spacing, and so on), also apply.

✔ The heading is typed centered in all caps 1 inch from the top of the page. The heading may also appear in boldface.

✔ The complexity of the report determines its length.

✔ Since the report may be desktop published in-house or printed professionally, your job of proofreading is especially critical.

Some of the principles of agreement are among the most commonly violated rules of grammar in business documents. Simple agreement of subject and verb *(She walks/They walk)* does not pose a problem for most writers. More obscure agreement errors *(The secretary in the corporate offices is)* are those which cause the writer and the proofreader to proceed very carefully.

Read the first page of the following report summary. Note the highlighted words. These illustrate three common errors in subject-verb agreement. Do you understand each error? You have the opportunity to review these very important grammar principles in this section of Chapter 4.

ENVIRONMENTALISTS AND THE LOGGING INDUSTRY

An Ongoing Debate in Need of Resolution

There **are** a growing concern within the general public and among environmentalists that the at-risk species debate, particularly the one surrounding the spotted owl, has lost its perspective. The questions we at Green Earth Inc. explored (under Federal Grant #3456-EV) were:

* What is the risk factor of the spotted owl?
* What, if any, industries are encroaching upon its natural habitat?
* Is the answer an either/or situation?
* Can the environmentalists and business interests co-exist?

Summary. The findings of the study conducted at Green Earth between September, 19XX, and April, 19XX, **indicates** that a peaceful resolution can be reached. The roots of the problem are deep. The infamous "bottom line" is survival. The owl must have the forest for its breeding and growth. Humans need the forests for jobs, particularly logging and fishing. The fact is that the forests that both man and owl **needs** for survival are almost gone.

PRINCIPLES AND PRACTICE
SUBJECT-VERB AGREEMENT

Agreement errors have been identified as one of the most frequent grammar errors appearing in business writing. Some errors in agreement of subject and verb are obvious. If a sentence reads, "The *collection are*...," you immediately recognize the error. However, when other words come between the subject and the verb, such as, "The *collection* of taxes from our southern and western regions *are* lagging," you might not spot the error because it "sounds" right.

The skilled proofreader, however, does recognize this type of error and corrects it. Your goal is to become just such a skilled person. Let's begin.

▼ PRINCIPLE 1: Agreement in Number

The basic rule of agreement is: The subject and verb must always agree in number.

• A singular subject must have a singular verb.

   She speaks persuasively.

• A plural subject must have a plural verb.

   The *interns plan* to meet tomorrow.

- Did you notice that singular verbs end in *s*?

- To determine whether a verb is singular or plural, read "he/she" (singular) or "they" (plural) in front of it. For example, is the verb *run* singular or plural? Is it correct to say, "he run" or "they run"? *They* is obviously correct; therefore, the plural verb is correct.

 PROOFREADING POINTERS

To reinforce your skill in checking subject-verb agreement, complete the following short exercise. Circle the correct verb in each of these sentences.

1. The engineers (is, are) playing in a tournament.
2. The new office buildings (looks, look) alike.
3. That printer (runs, run) quietly.
4. The support groups (meets, meet) on Tuesday mornings.
5. The copier (needs, need) repair.

Check your work in the Answer Key at the back of this book. If you selected the incorrect verb in any sentence, review your choice and indicate the correct one.

▼ PRINCIPLE 2: Compound Subjects

The second principle of agreement applies to compound subjects.

- Subjects joined by *and* require plural verbs.

  The secretary *and* the receptionist *are* new employees.

- Singular subjects joined by *or* require singular verbs.

  Either the secretary *or* the receptionist *is* new.

- If a singular subject and a plural subject are joined by *or* or *nor*, the verb agrees in number with the subject closer to it.

  The controller or the auditors *make* that decision.
  Neither the auditors nor the controller *makes* that decision.

Refer to Principle 2, and circle the correct verb in each of these sentences.

1. Neither the security person nor his personal guard (admit, admits) to seeing anything.
2. Your disk drives or your printer (is, are) probably malfunctioning.
3. Robotics and computer-assisted design (is, are) good courses to take in preparation for the future.
4. Marilyn and her two assistants (agree, agrees) to the change in work schedules.
5. Either Alaska or Texas (ranks, rank) first in area.

Check your work in the Answer Key. If you selected the incorrect verb in any sentence, review your choice and indicate the correct one.

▼ PRINCIPLE 3: Agreement of Pronouns and Verbs

A pronoun preceding or acting as the subject determines the number of the verb.

- Each, every. When a subject is preceded by *each* or *every*, the verb is always singular.

      Each of you *selects* your personal career path.
      Every suggestion *has* received individual attention.

- Indefinite pronouns are always followed by singular verbs. The most common indefinite pronouns are listed here.

another	everyone	one
anybody	everything	other
anyone	neither	somebody
anything	nobody	someone
either	no one	something
everybody	nothing	

      Everybody enjoys the same benefits.
      Someone is going to succeed.

- The pronoun *you* is always followed by a plural verb.

      You are an outstanding employee.
      You have my vote!

- A number, the number. The expression, *a number*, requires a plural verb; the expression, *the number*, takes a singular verb.

      A number of immigrants *have* excelled in astronomy.
      The number of respondents *was* small.

Refer to Principle 3, and circle the correct verb in each of the following sentences.

1. Anybody (is, are) welcome to attend the briefing.
2. You certainly (enjoys, enjoy) fine art.
3. The number of service technicians (is, are) growing.
4. Somebody (needs, need) to talk to Janine about her attitude.
5. Each employee (is, are) valued.

> *Check your work in the Answer Key. If you selected the incorrect verb in any sentence, review your choice and indicate the correct one.*

▼ PRINCIPLE 4: Find the Subject

Sometimes words other than the subject appear first in the sentence or come between the subject and the verb. These can cause confusion when you are trying to select the correct verb.

PROOFREADING POINTER		• Always be certain that you have identified the subject. If you have difficulty distinguishing the subject from other words in the sentence, use a simple diagram as shown below. The subject is a noun or pronoun that answers who, what, or where when placed in front of the verb.

My client travels to Europe frequently.

client   *travels*
 subject   verb

- <u>There and here</u>. *There* and *here* are adverbs and, as such, are never the subject of the sentence. Look for the subject elsewhere in the sentence.

  There *were* four *members* absent.
  Here *is* the missing *report*.
  There *are* many *reasons* for my reluctance to move ahead.

- <u>Intervening words</u>. One of the most confusing choices in agreement is having to select the verb when words come between the subject and the verb. Sometimes these are explanatory and may be in the form of a prepositional phrase. Again, you must find the simple subject and make certain that the simple subject and verb agree in number. Intervening phrases never determine the verb.

  The *catalog* containing all our items *is* in short supply.
  The *captain* of the office bowlers *is* a vivacious person.

Refer to Principle 4, and circle the correct verb in each of these sentences.

1. Here (is, are) my contributions to the effort.
2. The record levels of snowfall (makes, make) the test track hazardous.
3. There (was, were) bitter feelings after the harsh words.
4. The secretaries in our home office (rides, ride) on the motorcycle carelessly.
5. The total cost of the repairs (was, were) exorbitant.

Check your work in the Answer Key. If you selected the incorrect verb in any sentence, review your choice and indicate the correct one.

▼ PRINCIPLE 5: Collective Nouns 5-18 j

Nouns that name a group are called *collective nouns*.

- Since collective nouns refer to the group as a whole, they are usually singular. Here are some examples:

class	committee	*audience*
council	department	*jury*
group	staff	
team		

The *committee plans* to vote today on the location of the meeting.

- Proper nouns ending in *s* may appear plural. Usually, however, they are singular. Look at each of these examples.

> *Mason Brothers is* our major supplier.
> *Nelson and Jones is* the name of the law firm.
> *Consumer Reports is* a very popular magazine.

Refer to Principle 5, and circle the correct verb in each of these sentences.

1. McDougall and James (was, were) selected the outstanding law firm in the state.
2. The committee (was, were) voting on officers.
3. The management team (is, are) preparing a summary of the meeting.
4. Nadeau & Sons (sells, sell) more fruit than the next three retailers together.
5. The council (was, were) not in agreement on the next step.

> *Check your work in the Answer Key. If you selected the incorrect verb in any sentence, review your choice and indicate the correct one.*

5-18 L
5-18 F portions same for E.g.

Proof the following paragraphs from interoffice memos for agreement errors. Draw a line through each incorrect word, and write the correct form on the lines below each paragraph.

1. The four Thursday mornings in March presents a unique opportunity for the office support staff of the Sierra Health Network. Four outstanding training sessions, "You and Your Telephone," is to be presented in the High Sierra Conference Room.

    present   _are_
    line 1   line 4

2. Employees in office support level I or levels II and III is to register no later than Monday, May 15. The number of participants in these first four sessions are to be limited to 25. Each of the registrants are to complete the registration form individually.

    line 1 - are   line 4 - is
    line 3 - is

Check your work in the Answer Key.

Review the following paragraphs for errors in agreement. Draw a line through each incorrect word, and write the correct form on the lines below each paragraph.

1. McDonald, Harris, & Berowitz are the finest law firm in our area. This firm of 25 attorneys, with headquarters in the Sunrise Executive Plaza buildings, are our unanimous choice for legal representation for the next three years.

    line 1 - is
    line 3 - is

2. There is a number of reasons (see attachment) why we must deny your request. Most importantly, your reason for requesting an additional three vacation days do not meet the criteria in the Employee Agreement, Sec. IV, Par. 3.

    line 1 - are
    line 3 - does

Check your work in the Answer Key.

Unit Two concentrates on proofreading techniques for longer documents. While you will add to your proofreading ability by applying specific long-document techniques, you will also use the skills you acquired in Unit One. Proofreading is a cumulative skill—it grows with you as you become more skilled.

Proofreading long documents such as business reports:

1. Scan the document first.

   • Is there any way to make the document more readable?
   • Could more white space be added?
   • Could some information be made into lists or tables?

2. Make a style sheet to ensure consistency throughout a long document (see sample). Some of the notations you might list on your style sheet include:

   • Formatting of margins, headings, type fonts, etc.
   • Specialized vocabulary or jargon
   • Unusual capitalization or punctuation

   Make the style sheet work for you. Include those items that are typical of the documents you prepare.

```
PROOFREADER'S STYLE SHEET

Project:        _____

Originator:     _____

Date Due:       _____

Formatting:     _____



Text:



Graphics:
```

3. Proofread in steps. Check all titles and headings first.
4. Check the page numbers.
5. Read the body of the document for content and context. Ask yourself these questions:

- Are all words both used and spelled correctly?
- Does each sentence complete a thought and is it grammatically correct?

6. When keying from draft or edited copy, devise and follow a system to guarantee that all changes have been made in the final copy.

Document 1: Practice your proofreading skill by proofing part of the first page of the memo report that follows. Use proofreaders' marks to indicate errors.

Remember that formats of memo reports vary greatly among organizations. You may assume that your company uses the format illustrated on page 65-66.

```
TO:        Sales Representatives
FROM:      Jonathan Kindling
DATE:      September 3, 19XX
SUBJECT:   Consumer Purchasing Decisions


        It is well known that most cities have
several stores that carry similar merchandise.
Thus, consumers have a choice of stores in which to
make their purchases.  That choice is typically
influenced by such factors as quality, style, cost,
and location.  Knowing which of those factors is the
most important can make a difference in sales
results.

Summary.  The findings of surveys conducted in our
market areas indicate that often price is the only
consideration.  The fact that the consumer must
travel some distance, requiring time and cost, is
often ignored--when the price is right.

Background.  Recognizing that we have a superior
product, as we confirmed by independent testing
agencies, we wanted to learn why our sales figures
were constantly below projections.  In the national
market for our product, we ranked no higher than
fourth at any point during the past two years.  We
decided to use Klein & Roberts, a very successful
market research agency, to investigate this issue.
The method used by Kline & Roberts is described in
detail in Appendix A.
```

Document 2: Scan the following partial page of a memo report. Use the style sheet on page 78 and the format on pages 65-66 as your guides to formatting. Use proofreaders' marks to indicate errors in formatting.

```
FROM: Sharon Buckner
TO: Milton DeBruegge
DATE: August 15, 19XX
SUBJECT: Memo Report

             EMPOWERMENT FOR EMPLOYEES


        The latest buzzwords in offices across the
country are terms such as "empowerment,"
"teamwork," and "facilitators."  What do these
terms mean?  How are they applied?  Are they
effective?

Summary.  Management development specialists and
trainers are espousing a new form of participatory
management to address the needs of the "baby
boomers" who are in the job market today.  While
this form of management goes by many names, "team
builders" is probably the most common and the most
descriptive. Employees learn to ask, "What's the
problem?" and then go about solving it.

Background.  Organizational problems are common in
business; real solutions are less common.  One
approach to team building is through the use of
facilitators promoting team building among the
staff.  A frequently used approach is for a group
of employees to go on a retreat for the purpose of
getting in touch with themselves.  In the early
days of the team building movement, the questions
the participants grappled with were quite
personal.  The goal was to get to know themselves.
```

PROOFREADING ALERT

Punctuation marks such as commas and periods go inside quotation marks. This is not always the case with question marks. If the quote is a question (as shown at the end of the Summary paragraph in this document), the question mark goes inside the quotation mark. If the quote is not a question, but is in a sentence that is a question, the question mark goes outside the quotation mark. For example: Did you say "Come here"?

PROOFREADER'S STYLE SHEET

Project: *Memo Report: Empowerment*

Originator: *S. Buckner*

Date Due: *Aug. 18, 19XX*

Formatting: *Boldface title*
No # indentations
Italicize subheadings

Text: *"Ragged" right margins*

Correct spelling:
participatory management

Graphics:

none

Style Sheet for Document 2

Document 3: Proofread the following executive summary for errors in agreement of subject and verb. Use proofreaders' marks to indicate errors.

EXECUTIVE SUMMARY

The issues of depositor confidence and customer satisfaction is one of growing concern within the banking industry. American Savings Bank decided it was important to survey its customers to determine the degree of confidence and/or satisfaction they feel toward ASB. A sampling of the questions asked were:

* Is there any times when you worry about your deposits in ASB?
* How satisfied are you with the level of service you receive at ASB?
* Do you think your children will be better off than you are?
* Is the American dream still alive in your family?

To answer these questions, we organized 20 focus groups of 15 persons each, selected randomly from our family of customers. We were pleased to have a 78% acceptance rate to first-time invitations to participate.

The focus group concept, in its many variations, have been used very successfully within service industries of all types. The information we gained from the groups have already resulted in changes in our procedures: backup tellers for peak periods, increased hiring of part-time tellers for selected hours, improved audio systems for drive-in tellers.

Recommendation: Repeat the focus group experience in 18-24 months with new participants.

• When distributing copies of documents for review, use the redline and strikeout features of your software to indicate the latest changes. This eliminates the need for the reviewer to reread the entire document.

PROOFREADING POINTER

Document 4a: The proofreading process can be simplified if you use the capabilities of your word processing software when appropriate. The two features described here are particularly helpful (1) when several persons must proof the same document or (2) when the document is proofed several times before the final copy is prepared.

Document 4a has been proofread once; changes have been marked using the redline and strikeout features. Review the changes made to Document 4a.

LISTENING HABITS OF GREATER CINCINNATI LISTENERS
A Study Prepared for Stations WJRP, WABC, WEZL, and WVVB

The Greater Cincinnati area is one of the country's best radio audiences. We ~~have long~~ known that more people listen for longer periods of time in our area then in similar ~~typical~~ population areas anywhere else in the country. From that general knowledge, the four stations (WJRP, WABC, WEZL, and WVVB) asked Swartz Research Associates to conduct a more definitive survey of listening habits.

Findings. Over 82 percent of the respondents ~~asked~~ indicated that during the past seven days they had listened to Station A. (No stations will be identified by call letters.) The fewest number of respondents, less than 9 percent, listened to Station D.

The most frequent listening times was early morning, early evening, and late at night.

The largest percentage of listeners (57%) indicated that their musical preferences, in order of choice, was rock, country, and jazz.

The younger listeners (21 and under) listens most often after 10 p.m. More homemakers (63%) listen most often midday between 10 a.m. and 3 p.m.

Summary. Station A leads the ratings with the most listeners. The most popular listening times are from 5 a.m. to 10 a.m. and from 6 p.m. and 10 p.m. (often referred to as "drive time"). Rock is definitely the most popular type of music.

PROOFREADING POINTERS

▶

- Redlining highlights text that has been changed as illustrated in the following sentence. In this case, the redlined text has been added.

  Three of the four assistants (J. Keene, B. DeHaven, S. Ming, and K. Washington) have agreed to the change.

- Strikeout marks text to be deleted.

  Dan Greenhouse ~~of Detroit~~ has resigned effective immediately.

Note: The redline and strikeout features are printer dependent. The printed version produced by your printer may look different (for example, some printers use slashes rather than a straight delete line for strikeouts).

Document 4b: Document 4b was printed with the redline and strikeout corrections of Document 4a incorporated. Check that all corrections were made. Since there are additional errors, you need to proofread very carefully. Mark any errors you find.

Proofreaders commonly follow this procedure: First, clear an area on your work surface before you begin; this helps to minimize distractions. Then place documents in the best light. Third, place the original document at the left; the final copy always goes on the right. Finally, place a ruler or clean sheet of paper under the first line of text on each document and begin to read one line at a time.

```
        LISTENING HABITS OF GREATER CINCINNATI LISTENERS
     A Study Prepared for Stations WJRP, WABC, WEZL, and WVVB

          The Greater Cincinnati area is one of the
     country's best radio audiences.  We know that more people
     listen for longer periods of time in our area then in
     similiar population areas anywhere else in the country.
     From that general knowledge, the four stations (WJRP,
     WABC, WEZL, and WVVB) asked Swartz Research Associates to
     conduct a more definitive survey of listening habits.
     Findings.  Over 82 percent of the respondents indicated
     that during the past seven days they had listened to
     Station A. (No stations will be identified by call
     letters.)  The fewest number of respondents, less than 9
     percent, listened to Station D.
          The most frequent listening times was early
     morning, early evening, and late at night.
          The largest percentage of listeners (57%)
     indicated that their musical preferences, in order of
     choice, was rock, country, and jazz.
          The younger listeners (21 and under) listens most
     often after 10 p.m.  More homemakers (63%) listen most
     often midday between 10 a.m. and 3 p.m.
     Summary.  Station A leads the ratings with the most
     listeners. The most popular listening times are from 5
     a.m. to 10 a.m. and from 6 p.m. and 10 p.m. (often
     referred to as "drive time"). Rock is definately the most
     popular type of music.
```

Chapter 4 introduced you to formats for the body of business reports. Longer reports often include two additional major parts: front matter and end matter.

Front matter may include a letter of transmittal, cover or title page, table of contents, list of tables or figures, and preface.

End matter may include endnotes, a works-cited page, and appendixes.

This chapter concentrates on proofreading tables of contents, lists of figures, and works-cited pages:

- A table of contents lists the report's major sections and their page numbers. It is keyed after the report is complete.
- A list of figures lists the report's figures—charts, diagrams, and drawings—and their page numbers. It is also keyed after the report is complete.
- The works-cited page lists each source from which the writer borrowed information.

If you need formatting information on the other parts of business reports, you will find *The Paradigm Reference Manual* an excellent source.

Here are your goals for this chapter:

- Review formats for specific parts of business reports.
- Improve your skill in three language areas: correct choice of pronouns, agreement of pronouns and antecedents, and parallelism.
- Continue to develop your skill in proofreading for both format and content.

Unlike the body of business reports, the report parts covered in this section are fairly standard. When you complete this section, you will feel quite confident that you can proofread these sections of longer reports.

TABLE OF CONTENTS

```
                      TABLE OF CONTENTS

                                                    Page

LIST OF FIGURES  . . . . . . . . . . . .   iii
PREFACE   . . . . . . . . . . . . . . .    iv
SUMMARY  . . . . . . . . . . . . . . .      1
BACKGROUND . . . . . . . . . . . . . .      2
          Situation . . . . . . . . . .     2
          Problem Statement . . . . . . .   4
FINDINGS . . . . . . . . . . . . . . .      5
          Regional Prospects  . . . . . .   6
          National Prospects  . . . . . .   7
          International Prospects . . . . . 8
CONCLUSION . . . . . . . . . . . . . .      9
RECOMMENDATIONS  . . . . . . . . . . .     10
FOLLOW-UP  . . . . . . . . . . . . . .     11
WORKS CITED  . . . . . . . . . . . . .     12
APPENDIX . . . . . . . . . . . . . . .     13




                         ii
```

PROOFREADING ALERT
Always read each item listed in a table of contents against the most up-to-date version of the report.

FORMATTING CHECKPOINTS

✔ Check that the table of contents uses the same margins as the report.
✔ Check that the heading TABLE OF CONTENTS is centered 1 to 2 inches from the top of the page. The length of the table of contents determines your top margin.

✔ Triple-space after the heading; key *Page* flush right.

✔ Double-space and begin the list of sections.

✔ Key major sections of the report in all caps. Indent subsections and use initial caps only. Note that the sections shown here are examples only. The sections will vary with the contents of the report.

✔ Use leaders (...) to guide the reader's eye to the page number.

✔ Use lowercase Roman numerals to number front matter pages.

✔ Generate a table of contents easily by using a full-feature word processing software program.

LIST OF FIGURES

```
                     LIST OF FIGURES


Figure                                          Page

1. Average Annual Pay Increase  . . . . . . . . .  3
2. Percent of Budget Spent on Salaries  . . . . .  7
3. Average Salary Compared with Competitors'  . . 12
4. Average Annual Pay Increase by Department  . . 19
5. Increase in Percent of Budget Spent on Benefits . 22
```

PROOFREADING ALERT

Compare figure titles to the titles that appear on the actual figures.

Follow the same format as the table of contents with the following modifications:

✔ Key *Figure* at the left margin on the same line as *Page*.

✔ Key the number of each figure at the left margin, then the title of the figure.

✔ Number figures consecutively throughout the report or within each chapter or section. When numbered separately in each section, the section number should precede the figure number; for example, Figure 2-3.

✔ Include the list of tables before the list of figures on a separate page when a report includes several tables and several figures.

WORKS-CITED PAGE(S)

```
                        WORKS CITED

Bartholomew, J.   Personal Law and You.   New York:
     Legal P, 1992.

"Just When We Thought It Was Safe."   The Financial
     Journal 6 (1993): 12-14.

Largent, R.L.   "Forgotten Customers."   American Legal
     Journal 9 (1992): 14-21.

Peterson, F., and J. Baily.   A Lawyer's Casebook.
     Eden Prairie, MN: EMC, 1993.

Venduzi, C.   Keynote Address.   Twenty-fifth Annual
     Meeting of Midwest Lawyers.   Chicago, Dec. 19-21,
     1994.
```

FORMATTING CHECKPOINTS

✔ Use the same margins as the report.
✔ Center the title WORKS CITED 2 inches from the top of the page.
✔ Arrange the citations alphabetically by author.
✔ Position the first line of each citation at the left margin. Indent all subsequent lines one tab stop. (Your software may have a hanging indent tab.)
✔ Italicize or underline book, magazine, and journal titles. Use quotation marks with article and speech titles.

Refer to the table of contents format on pages 84-85, and scan the following table of contents. Use proofreaders' marks to indicate any format errors.

Table of Contents

Page

Check your work in the Answer Key at the back of this book.

USING LANGUAGE EFFECTIVELY
PRONOUNS AND PARALLELISM

Read the following list of figures. Note the highlighted words. These illustrate five common errors in pronoun usage and parallelism. Do you understand each error? This section reviews pronouns and parallelism for you.

```
                          LIST OF FIGURES

       Figure                                            Page
```

The review of pronouns will include two basic principles:

1. Using the correct pronoun: Is "Jane and *I* will attend the seminar" correct? Or is it "Jane and *me*"?
2. Applying agreement to pronouns and their *antecedents*, the words to which pronouns refer, as in "John repaired his printer." *John* is the antecedent of the pronoun *his*.

PRINCIPLES AND PRACTICE

PRONOUNS

Let's begin this section by reviewing correct pronoun usage.

▼ PRINCIPLE 1: The Correct Case

Using the right pronoun is dependent on an understanding of the case, or form, of pronouns. You may recall that pronouns may be either nominative, objective, or possessive case. Each case has a specific use in a sentence.

Nominative case. The *nominative case* pronouns are *I, we, you, he, she, it, they,* and *who.* The nominative case is used in two ways:

1. When the pronoun is the subject.

    She is my choice for the new position.

2. When the pronoun follows a linking verb: *is, are, am, was, were, be,* and *been.* (When the pronoun follows a linking verb, it is called a *predicate nominative.*)

    It was *he* who made the original recommendation.

Objective case. *5-7c*
    The *objective case* pronouns are *me, us, you, him, her, it, them,* and *whom.* The objective case is used in two ways:

    1. When the pronoun is the object of a verb.

        The malfunctioning printer baffled *her.*

    2. When the pronoun is the object of a preposition.

        Please give the refund to *me.*

Remember that the object answers the question "who" or "what" after the verb.

Possessive case. *5-7d*
    The *possessive case* pronouns are *my, mine, our, ours, your, yours, his, her, hers, its, their, theirs,* and *whose.* The possessive case is used to show ownership. Do not use an apostrophe with a possessive pronoun.

    Can you determine *its* value?
    Their office is next to *mine.*

---

* One of the most often misused pronouns is *its.* The form *it's* is a contraction and is used only when *it is* or *it has* can be substituted. "It's a step forward!" can also be stated as "It is a step forward!" and is, therefore, correct.

◄ PROOFREADING POINTER

Circle the correct pronoun form in each of the following ten sentences.

1. Her reply, "It is (I, me)," surprised all of us.
2. The floor manager asked (we, us) to assist him.
3. The impatient representative left (she, her) catalogs on the desk.
4. Shall (we, us) talk another time?
5. (They, Them) wanted more time to make the decision.

6. Lisa purchased a thoughtful gift for (he, <u>him</u>).
7. (<u>It's</u>, Its) the receptionist's job to distribute mail.
8. Mr. Chavez agreed with (we, <u>us</u>) on most points.
9. The principal speaker will be (<u>she</u>, her).
10. He will agree to meet with (we, <u>us</u>).

> *Check your work in the Answer Key. If you selected the incorrect pronoun in any sentence, review your choice and indicate the correct one.*

▼ PRINCIPLE 2: Using Pronouns with Compounds and after *Than* or *As*

- Selecting the correct pronoun when it is a part of a compound subject or object can be confusing. Principle #1 for selecting the correct case still applies: Nominative case pronouns are used as subjects or predicate nominatives; objective case pronouns are used as objects of verbs or prepositions.

  There is a simple test that you can apply to make the right choice. Cross out the other component of the compound, for example:

  ~~Sally and~~ (I, me) are taking a management course.

  Would you now select *I* or *me*? [I (am) taking a management course. *or* Me (am) taking a management course.] *I* is quickly revealed as the subject of the sentence and is your choice. The same test can be used for objects:

  Do you believe he did this just for ~~you and~~ (I, me)?

  Would you say for *I* ? Again, the answer is obvious; you select *me* as object of the preposition *for*.

PROOFREADING POINTER ▶

- One of the most frequently misused expressions is *between you and I*. In fact, you will hear many public speakers use it. After studying this section, you will realize that the correct pronoun is *me* as the object of the preposition *between*.

- When a personal pronoun follows the word *as* or *than*, choose the correct case by mentally inserting the missing words.

    Kerry is the same age as (she, her).

This may be read as: Kerry is the same age as she [is]. *She* is acting as the subject of a clause.

    Mail it to Todd rather than (I, me).

This may be read as: Mail it to Todd rather than [to] me. *Me* is acting as the object of the preposition *to*.

Circle the correct pronoun in each of these sentences.

1. Marty led a tour of the test site for (they, <u>them</u>).
2. The coordinator of the civic project was (<u>she</u>, her).
3. This discussion should be kept between you and (I, <u>me</u>).
4. No one knows the importance of education better than (<u>I</u>, me).
5. It was not Juan who was at fault, it was (<u>he</u>, him).
6. The president and (<u>she</u>, her) rewrote the bylaws.
7. It was (<u>she</u>, her) who made the inflammatory statement.
8. Do you want to go as badly as (<u>I</u>, me)?
9. My staff members and (<u>I</u>, me) are flying to the conference.
10. It was (<u>they</u>, them) who made the arrangements.

Check your work in the Answer Key. If you selected the incorrect pronoun in any sentence, review your choice and indicate the correct one.

▼ PRINCIPLE 3: Agreement in Number and Gender

The noun to which a pronoun refers is called the *antecedent*.

    Denise submitted her resignation to Peter Chin.
    The pronoun is *her*; the antecedent is *Denise.*

- A pronoun must always agree in number with its antecedent. When applicable, a pronoun must also agree in gender, or sex.

    The *salesman* reached *his* quota. (both singular and masculine)

    The *members* of the Jones family are planning *their* family reunion. (both plural)

- Formerly the masculine gender was used when the antecedent applied to persons of both sexes. That practice is no longer considered acceptable. There are three ways of ensuring that your documents do not contain sexist references.

   1. Use both masculine and feminine gender pronouns.

      Each *employee* must file *his or her* own report.

   While this might be acceptable for a single occurrence, it can become quite cumbersome if there are several references within a document.

   2. Change the antecedent and pronoun from singular to plural.

      All *employees* must file *their* own reports.

   This eliminates the reference to gender, but it can sometimes be awkward and fail to express the intended meaning.

   3. Rewrite the sentence to avoid the use of a pronoun.

      Reports must be filed by individual employees.

   This is the recommended solution.

▼ **PRINCIPLE 4: Indefinite Pronouns and Compound Antecedents**

- Some indefinite pronouns are singular: *each, every, either, neither, one, another,* and *much*.

   Each person must bring *his or her* own notes to the meeting. (Refer to Principle 3 for other ways of writing this sentence.)

- When a prepositional phrase follows an indefinite pronoun, the prepositional phrase is not the antecedent and, therefore, does not determine the number of the pronoun.

   Each of the female students was asked to list *her* first name.

- When two or more antecedents are joined by the word *and,* a plural pronoun is used.

Margaret and Michael gave *their* status report.
When *Johanna and her assistants* arrive, *they* will be surprised.

Refer to Principles 3 and 4, and circle the correct pronoun in each of these sentences.

1. Each male employee must specify (his, their) draft status.
2. The dean and his associates said (he, they) would be unable to complete the project this week.
3. Doctors Mackle and Thurmond completed (his, her, their) hospital rounds in less than two hours.
4. All secretaries are to begin (his, her, their) working day at eight o'clock.
5. Every company must balance (its, their) books.

Check your work in the Answer Key. If you selected the wrong pronoun in any sentence, review the principle governing the choice.

PRINCIPLES AND PRACTICE
PARALLELISM

Related items should be grammatically consistent. In other words, adjectives should be parallel with adjectives, nouns with nouns, as shown in the following examples. This is referred to as *parallel structure* or *parallelism*.

The left-hand column in the following table illustrates parallel structure. The first two examples focus on parts of speech: adjectives and gerunds (verbs ending in *-ing* acting as nouns). For comparison, the right-hand column illustrates the same item or sentence with faulty parallel structure. Study each example carefully.

Correct	Faulty
Adjectives in a series:	
The meeting was *brief, intensive,* and *productive*.	The meeting was *brief, intensive*, and *produced* results.
Gerunds:	
Your duties will include telephon*ing*, fil*ing*, and greet*ing* visitors.	Your duties will include telephon*ing*, fil*ing,* and receptionist.
Outline:	
I. Types of Spreadsheets	I. Types of Spreadsheets
A. Single Function	A. Single Function
B. Integrated Package	B. Integrated Package
II. The *Uses* of Spreadsheets	II. *Using* Spreadsheets

Grammatical structure must also be parallel when *correlative adjectives* are used. Common correlative adjectives are *either/or, neither/nor, not only/but also, both/and,* and *whether/or.*

Correct	**Faulty**
They planned not only to *interview* me on the 26th but also to *hire* me.	They planned not only to *interview* me on the 26th but also *hiring* me.
Neither *rest* nor *exercise* improved her condition.	Neither *rest* nor *doing exercises* improved her condition.

Proofread each of these sentences for errors in parallel structure. Use proofreaders' marks to correct the sentences.

1. Send a copy of the letter both to John Avery and Iva Gray.
2. My new duties include preparing the accounts, balancing the worksheets, and budgets. *budgeting*
3. Neither improving her skills nor a promise *ing* to arrive on time will save her job at this point.
4. Alison not only wrote the report but also is typing it. *typed*
5. The subheadings of the report are:

   Determining Our Purpose
   Refining Our Goals
   Achievement of Our Goals *Achieving*

Check your work in the Answer Key.

MASTERY CHECKPOINT ONE

Proof these paragraphs for errors in pronoun usage. Draw a line through the incorrect pronouns, and write the correct ones on the lines below each paragraph.

1. The state negotiator agreed to meet with the union officers and I on May 1. Its imperative that you and I meet before that date. I know you want this issue resolved as much as me. Since it was them who requested the meeting, I think the possibility is good.

   (1) *me*   (3) *I*
   (2) *It's*   (4) *They*

2. Dean gave the report to Carlita and I on Friday. Carlita hopes to meet with he and Mr. Weinstein on Monday. Do you think you could attend rather than me? Just between you and I, I think you are better informed about the matter.

   (1) *me*   (3) *I*
   (2) *him*   (4) *me*

Check your work in the Answer Key.

94 ■ PROOFREADING LONG BUSINESS DOCUMENTS

Proof the following paragraphs for errors in agreement of pronouns and antecedents. Draw a line through the incorrect pronouns, and write the correct forms on the lines below each paragraph.

1. The committee has decided to review their findings on the environmental impact of the testing. Each of the members is to review his own position. Everyone is to then submit the results of their second review to Sandi Kyte.

   ① *its*   ③ *the*

   ② *his or her*

2. Each doctor on staff performs in his own unique manner. Likewise, each nurse brings her own personality to the job. The result is a team that functions very smoothly. Everyone can be proud that he is a member of the Sunrise team!

   ① *a his or her*

   Check your work in the Answer Key.

Proof the following paragraphs for errors in parallelism. Draw a line through any text that is not parallel with its related text. Write the correct parallel form on the lines below each paragraph.

1. The supervisor was having difficulty deciding whether he should promote Elizabeth Cantor or to transfer her to another department. Greeting people is one of her strengths but to file accurately is one of her weaknesses.

   _____   _____

   _____   _____

2. The consultants studied the proposals and how they were developed. The process included conducting a needs assessment, setting program goals, and measurement of outcomes.

   _____   _____

   _____   _____

   Check your work in the Answer Key.

Proofreading front and end matter of business reports involves very detailed reading. Since these sections are prepared after the body of the report, the proofreading process becomes very important. Often these parts are keyed on another day; the time lapse only adds to the critical nature of your task.

Proofreading front matter of long documents:

1. Align continuing lines of indented text at the tab—not the left margin. If you are using word processing software and use the indent feature rather than a tab, this will occur automatically.
2. Double-check page number references. If you have added text or graphics, other parts of the document may have shifted.
3. Check the sequence of sections.
4. Compare the wording of each section or chapter title with the item in the report. It is easy to transpose or omit words.

Proofreading end matter of long documents:

1. Check the accuracy of all listings. Particularly check the spelling of dates and the accuracy of numbers.
2. Check the accuracy of all appendix references within the text.

Document 1: The format of this table of contents has some inconsistencies. Review the Formatting Checkpoints on page 85. Use proofreaders' marks to indicate errors.

```
        TABLE OF CONTENTS


LIST OF FIGURES . . . . . . . . . . . . . . . . II
        Preface   . . . . . . . . . . . . . . . IV
        Summary   . . . . . . . . . . . . . . .  1
        Background  . . . . . . . . . . . . . .  2
        Findings  . . . . . . . . . . . . . . .  4
                Personnel   . . . . . . . . . .  6
                Finance   . . . . . . . . . . .  8
                Strategic Planning  . . . . . . 10
        CONCLUSION  . . . . . . . . . . . . . . 12
        RECOMMENDATIONS   . . . . . . . . . . . 15
WORKS CITED   . . . . . . . . . . . . . . . . . 20
```

Document 2: Scan the following works-cited page. Refer to the format on page 86, as necessary. Use proofreaders' marks to indicate errors in formatting.

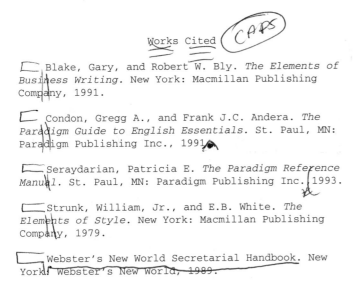

Works Cited ~~Works Cited~~ (CAPS)

Blake, Gary, and Robert W. Bly. *The Elements of Business Writing.* New York: Macmillan Publishing Company, 1991.

Condon, Gregg A., and Frank J.C. Andera. *The Paradigm Guide to English Essentials.* St. Paul, MN: Paradigm Publishing Inc., 1991.

Seraydarian, Patricia E. *The Paradigm Reference Manual.* St. Paul, MN: Paradigm Publishing Inc. 1993.

Strunk, William, Jr., and E.B. White. *The Elements of Style.* New York: Macmillan Publishing Company, 1979.

Webster's New World Secretarial Handbook. New York: Webster's New World, 1989.

Document 3: Proofread the following paragraph for errors in pronoun usage and agreement. Use proofreaders' marks to indicate errors.

A Note from the Desk of TOM HOFMEISTER

I am suggesting that you add the following end matter to the fine report you have written: the usual endnotes, work-cited page, and ~~then prepare~~ three appendixes (see attached page).

Otherwise, it is possible that a manager in any one of our regions may claim that ~~his~~ the report does not contain supporting information. You will recall that Marcia Yantz raised that very issue last year. Just between you and ~~I~~ me, I think you have presented adequate evidence throughout the report; but it's essential that no more time be lost rewriting any portion of it.

Again, the teamwork of Westar comes through. Normally, the final proofreading would be done by Donald Lewis. Since Don was involved in the writing, the proofreading will be done by Anna Kotsch rather than ~~he~~ him. The administrative staff of the Denver office has offered to oversee the printing and distribution for you and ~~I~~ me.

me

Document 4: Proofread the following document for any errors in format or language covered in Chapters 1 to 5. Use proofreaders' marks to indicate errors.

memorandum

To: Corporate PR Crew   **From:**   Barbara Lombardi
Date: July 27, 19XX   **Subject:** Annual Report

      Oh joy! It's all ready that time again--
annual report planning time.   These are my initial
thoughts:

    Aug. 15:   First planning session
    Aug. 30:   Begin writing
    Sept. 15:   First draft completed
    Sept. 30:   Final copy completed
    Oct. 1:   Proofread final copy
    Oct. 5:   Final copy to printer
    Oct. 15:   Distribution of report in-
                    house

How does these dates strike you? Is it
achievable?

When each of you people have had a chance to
consider this schedule, please register "Yea" or
"Nay" on my voice mail by August 5. Shannon and
me will make the planning meeting arrangements.

nbn

Document 5: Endnotes are another type of end matter of business reports. Endnotes are used when the writer wants to comment on information in the report or provide additional information. Each endnote is keyed to the information in the body of the report.

You may assume that the format shown is correct. Proofread the endnotes for errors in language.

ENDNOTES

1. Largent also points out that many public school systems provides simple legal services for students but that lawyers function under severe limitations. First, they provide only minimal services, such as advise on handling small claims court actions. Thus, when students need further assistants, including court appearances, these school lawyers can only refer them to others, who than charge for services. Second, a school-supplied lawyer often maintains a private practice and is paid little for their service to school. Thus, students may question the real dedication of these lawyers to his nonpaying school clientele. In some cases, conflict of interest charges has arisen when a lawyer, operating as an adviser in the schools, his or her has refered students to their own legal service or to a friendly service. For the purposes of this study then these part-time legal advisory services provided by schools are not considered legal services because of their limitations.

Chapters 4 and 5 introduced you to proofreading the major sections of business reports. Chapter 6 refines your knowledge of business reports and presents additional formatting guidelines for multipage reports. This chapter covers:

- Headers and footers. A brief header or footer is keyed on each page of a long report to remind readers which section they are reading. The header may include the title of the report or may be the section heading.
- Page numbers.
- Page breaks.

Here are your goals for this chapter:

- Review guidelines for formatting special parts of multipage reports.
- Refine your language skills in two areas: the correct choice of adjectives and verbs.
- Continue developing your skill in proofreading for both format and content.

Many companies have standard formats for *continuation pages* (the second and following pages) of reports. In such cases, of course, you should adhere to those formats. In the absence of such standards, this chapter will help you develop a set of consistent formats for longer reports.

HEADERS

```
Employee Benefits Staff
Page 2
August 30, 19XX


insurance benefits to be paid for pre-existing
conditions. These will be subject to the review of
the Medical Review Staff.
```

```
Employee Benefits Staff    Page 2       August 30, 19XX


insurance benefits to be paid for pre-existing
conditions. These will be subject to the review of
the Medical Review Staff.
```

FORMATTING CHECKPOINTS

✔ Include the name of the addressee, the page number, and the date of the report.
✔ Use the same margins as in the report.
✔ Generally begin the heading 1 inch from the top of the page.
✔ Triple-space to resume the body of the report.

FOOTERS

```
the breakdown in the communication process was
unfortunate but not irreparable.

September 30, 19XX                        HRQTRREP
```

SAMPLE FOOTER WITH DATE AND FILE NAME

FORMATTING CHECKPOINT

✔ Footers may be used to show other important information such as the date of the report and the file name.

PAGE NUMBERS

```
   APPENDIXES  . . . . . . . . . . . . . . . . . . .21

                            ii
```

SAMPLE PAGE NUMBERING OF FRONT MATTER

```
   and develop a spirit of teamwork within your
   department, your work group, or your organization.

                            4
```

SAMPLE PAGE NUMBERING FOR BODY OF REPORT

```
   Continuing Education - Page 2


   to be offered during the Winter term, 19XX.  Call
   Carol Kenski in HR (X345) for more information.
```

SAMPLE PAGE NUMBERING IN HEADER

FORMATTING CHECKPOINTS

✔ Number front matter pages at the bottom with centered, lowercase Roman numerals (ii, iii, iv); count the title page as page i but do not print the page number on it.

✔ Begin numbering the body of the report on the first page of text. Use Arabic numerals and number continuously, including any end matter.

✔ <u>Numbering at the top</u>: Key page numbers 1 inch from the top of the page. Resume keying the text on the third line below the page number.

✔ <u>Numbering at the bottom</u>: Decrease the bottom margin to 0.5 inches and key the page number on that line. The text of the report should still end 1 inch from the bottom of the page.

✔ Apply these guidelines for placement of page numbers when you include page numbers within a header or footer.

✔ Use the page numbering feature of your software to number pages automatically. It renumbers pages whenever you add or delete text or graphics.

PAGE BREAKS

> Continuing Education - Page 10
>
> The students who learn at a faster pace are expected to excel as their interest pulls them into different and more advanced areas of expertise.

✔ Never leave a single line of a paragraph at the top or bottom of any page.

✔ Avoid page breaks that separate blocks of text such as indented quotations, lists, tables, or other figures.

✔ Avoid dividing words or related words such as figures, dates, or names at the bottom of a page.

✔ Use the *widow/orphan feature* of your software. This feature automatically places at least two lines of a paragraph on the bottom or top of any page.

✔ Use the *block protect feature* of your software to keep blocks of text together.

Scan the following footer and header for accuracy of format. Use proofreaders' marks to indicate any format errors.

> the task of making a newsletter readable. Most readers like lots of white space, lots of graphics, a
>
> Page 10

> George Kovale   September 15, 19XX   Page 2
>
> rupted plans for the next meeting are incomplete. Ashley will call you when she has further information.

Check your work in the Answer Key at the back of this book.

Read the following conclusion of a business report. Note the highlighted words. These illustrate five common errors in the use of adjectives and verbs. Do you understand each error? This section will help you sharpen your language skills in these two areas.

Conclusion. Of the three alternatives, Proposal 2 is definitely the **better**. Proposal 1 **has went** too far toward addressing all problem areas. Proposal 3 is the **most unique** but fails to address the critical issue. Proposal 2 is the **more feasible** and will reassure those who **seen** this problem coming.

4

PRINCIPLES AND PRACTICE

ADJECTIVES

Adjectives are very important parts of our language. In their role as modifiers of nouns and pronouns, they help our language come alive. Consider the simple sentence: "The secretary is capable." Are you apt to ask, "What secretary?" Or, "In what areas is she most capable?" Consider the same sentence with adjectives: "The Employee Relations secretary is a skilled word processor and an excellent communicator." Three adjectives, *Employee Relations*, *skilled*, and *excellent*, provide a mental picture of the secretary. Such adjectives are known as *modifiers*.

▼ PRINCIPLE 1: Comparative and Superlative Forms

Adjectives have two additional forms: the *comparative* and the *superlative*. While you may not recall these labels, you are already familiar with them. Consider the following adjectives.

Modifier	Comparative Form	Superlative Form
great	greater	greatest
pretty	prettier	prettiest
profitable	more profitable	most profitable

Each of these forms has specific uses.

Comparative Form

- Form the comparative by adding *-er*, *more*, or *less* to the adjective. How you form the comparative is generally determined by the ease of pronunciation. Whenever you are in doubt, consult your dictionary.

- Use the comparative form when comparing two things:

    This year's sales were *higher* than last year's.
    Product A is *more popular* than Product B.

Superlative Form

- Form the superlative by adding *-est*, *most*, or *least* to the adjective.

- Use the superlative form when comparing three or more things:

    This year's sales are the *highest* of the past ten years.
    Product A is the *most popular* of the five similar ones.

Exceptions
A few adjectives form the comparative and superlative by changing form.

bad	worse	worst
good	better	best
little	less	least
many	more	most

Circle the correct adjective form in each of these sentences.

1. Of the two colors, this one is the (brighter, brightest).
2. Your method is certainly the (more, most) efficient of the two.
3. Your proposal was obviously the (better, best) of the four submitted.
4. Of the two positions open, which one interests you (more, most)?
5. This decision is the (harder, hardest) I have ever had to make.

Check your work in the Answer Key. If you selected the incorrect adjective in any sentence, review Principle 1.

PRINCIPLE 2: Troublesome Comparisons

▼

Here are two additional refinements in the use of adjectives that you should be aware of.

- Avoid double comparisons.

    Wrong: Your diet is the *most* healthiest I have ever known.
    Right: Your diet is the healthi*est* I have ever known.

- Some adjectives should not be compared for logical reasons.

    round   perfect   empty   unique

- Still, adverbs such as *more/most* and *less/least* can be applied to these.

    Wrong: Your solution is *more perfect* than Clyde's.
    Right: Your solution is *more nearly perfect* than Clyde's.

Read each of these sentences carefully. Correct any errors you find in adjective use.

1. Supplies are ~~more~~ cheaper at Office Biz.
2. Our goal is to do a more complete study next year.
3. The new fountain in the courtyard is ~~more~~ taller than the old one.
4. The meeting was definitely ~~more~~ shorter than the previous one.
5. Your opinion is the least kind~~est~~ I have heard.

Check your work in the Answer Key. If you missed the incorrect adjective in any sentence, review Principle 2.

PRINCIPLES AND PRACTICE

VERBS

Verbs are among the most familiar parts of speech. Even people who have difficulty identifying the parts of speech can usually identify the verb in a sentence. Verbs are classified as one of two types: *regular* or *irregular*.

▼ PRINCIPLE 1: Regular Verbs

Regular verbs form the past tense and past participle by adding -*d* or -*ed*.

Present tense	Past tense	Past participle
employ	employed	employed
compute	computed	computed

▼ PRINCIPLE 2: Irregular Verbs

Irregular verbs form the past tense and past participle by changing form.

Present tense	Past tense	Past participle
see	saw	seen
go	went	gone

The past participle must always have a *helping verb*. A helping verb is an auxiliary word: *is, are, am, was, were, has, have, had, can, could, do, did, may, might, must, shall, will, should,* and *could.*

Past tense: I *saw* the doctor twice last week.
Past participle: I *have seen* the doctor twice in the last week.

PROOFREADING POINTER ▶

* Refer to your dictionary whenever you are in doubt about the past participle form. The past tense and past participle forms are listed immediately following the base word.

Circle the correct verb form in each of these sentences.

1. The client had already (spoke, spoken) to the director about the matter.
2. Have you (begun, began) to make your vacation plans?
3. My staff has (gone, went) to the conference for many years.
4. I heard that Maria always (did, done) her share.
5. The fired employee had deliberately (hid, hidden) the records.

Check your work in the Answer Key. If you selected the incorrect verb in any sentence, review the verb principles.

Proof the following paragraphs for errors in the use of adjectives. Draw a line through the incorrect adjectives, and write the correct forms on the lines below each paragraph.

1. I have just completed the review of the ~~most~~ finest sales campaign we have ever conducted. Of the top two territories, Midwest and Mountain Plains, the Midwest had ~~the most~~ sales. Of the next three territories, the South had ~~more~~ sales.

   ① delete most   ③ the most
   ② more

2. Which of you has the ~~highest~~ salary? I need to do a ~~more~~ total review of everyone's salary history. Since you are two of the ~~more older~~ employees, I think you are a good starting point. Is it ~~best~~ to interview you or to conduct a review of your records?

   ① higher   ③ older
   ② delete more   ④ better

Check your work in the Answer Key.

Proof the following paragraphs for errors in verbs. Draw a line through any verb that is incorrect. Write the correct verb on the lines below each sample.

1. The technicians have ~~came~~ three times this week and have ~~did~~ their best to correct the "bug" in our systems. We have ~~began~~ to think the problem cannot be corrected. We are very disappointed because these computers were carefully chosen after comparison shopping.

   ① come   ③ begun
   ② done   ④ chosen

2. Public Act 489 has ~~laid~~ on Lucinda Dey's congresswoman's desk for more than 90 days. Lucinda Dey has ~~wrote~~ to her expressing her feelings in the matter. She is so incensed she wishes she had ~~flew~~ to Washington on her recent business trip to Philadelphia.

   ① lain   ③ flown
   ② written

Check your work in the Answer Key.

Reading the special parts of business reports requires continued attention to detail. You might consider checking continuation pages "the finishing touch" in the proofreading process. When you have completed this section, you will feel very confident that you have a completely accurate document.

Proofreading headers and footers:

1. Scan the placement of headers and footers on all applicable pages because a single word processing command, inadvertently inserted, may change the position or content.
2. If you have issued a "discontinue" command on any page, check to be sure the header or footer resumes on the next applicable page.

Proofreading page numbers:

1. Before compiling a report for distribution, check the page numbers on all pages. A malfunction of the printer may omit a page.
2. If pages are numbered by sections, check that each new section begins on the correct page.
3. Generally, the page number font should match the text. It should never distract from the text because of its style or size.

Proofreading page breaks:

1. If you turned on the widow/orphan feature, you should not have any single lines at the bottoms or tops of pages.
2. Use the block protect feature to keep related items such as lists, tables, and graphics on the same page.

Document 1: Review the following text for continuation page errors. Use proofreaders' marks to indicate errors.

Sensitivity Training   Page 4

Will conclude our efforts to educate and inform our
staff in the important areas of sensitivity to
others.

---

three questionable incidents that prompted the
inquiry and study.

The first of these incidents may be described as:

Page 5

Document 2: Scan the following partial pages of a business report for consistency of format. Review the formatting checkpoints as needed. Use proofreaders' marks to indicate format errors.

APPENDIX A 23

APPENDIX B 24

Page 2

FRONT MATTER

Employment Planning
Page 5

number of new hires, percentage of temporary
employees, and anticipated number of terminations.

HEADER

Masters' Concert Series   Page 7

to conclude with the Vienna Symphony.

No single line on page

PAGE BREAKS

Document 3: Proofread the following paragraphs for errors in the use of adjectives and verbs. Use proofreaders' marks to indicate errors.

McAllister Foundation

During the last twelve months contributors have ~~gave~~ *given* over $50,000 to the Fund. This is the ~~most~~ largest amount given in a single year to date.

We think the fact that we have ~~went~~ *gone* from taxable to tax-exempt status played an important role in this achievement. Of our three largest donors, Midwest Gas, Borzone Corporation, and Wichita Chemicals, Midwest Gas gave the ~~larger~~ *largest* amount--$10,000.

We also now have the ~~most~~ finest records of any foundation in the state. We are very proud of that!

What is our next major step? It could be any one of three: (1) to network our computer system; (2) to hire a full-time director of community services; or (3) to move to larger facilities. We think No. 1 is the ~~more~~ *most* likely to occur.

Document 4: The following page from a business report may contain errors from any of the material covered in Chapters 1 to 6. Follow these proofreading steps:

1. Scan the document for formatting consistency.
2. Read the document for errors in language skills.

The Feasibility of Providing Student Legal Services ~ CAPS

Legal professionals and lay people alike share a genuine concern over the unavailability of legal services for students.

THE PROBLEM: Since a large majority of students in any institution of higher learning are legal adults, but are often uncertain of his/her [their] legal rights and obligations, a study should be conducted to investigate the feasibility of employing a lawyer for the students.

Statement of the Problem. The purposes of this study is [are] to: (1) determine the amount of need for legal services by students, (2) survey the desire for and attitudes toward this proposal by a representative sample of the student body and faculty, (3) discover the workability of such a program, and (4) finally, determining what services should be provided. *The Financial Journal,* along with several other similar publications, sight [cite] a survey of 1,200 New York students in which 25% reported they had encountered legal problems. Only 3.5% had ever spoke [spoken] to a lawyer, and 1.1% had retained council. [sp]

This seems to be an indicator that, although the need is present, few people recieve the legal attention neccessary for their problems.

(margin note: take on stmt)

PROOFREADING ALERT

Certain expressions may be represented in words or symbols, such as percent (%), at (@), or number (#). Either the word or the symbol should be used consistently. Sometimes you may find that the words are used in the narrative section of the document, and the symbol is used in tables or graphics. This is acceptable, as long as the usage is consistent.

PROOFREADING MULTIPAGE REPORTS ■ 113

PERFORMANCE GOALS

UPON COMPLETING THIS UNIT, YOU WILL BE ABLE TO:

- Correct formats of envelopes and mailing labels according to U.S. Postal Service standards

- Correct the format of tables in business documents to enhance readability

- Interpret graphs to verify accuracy of information

- Proofread for correct application of punctuation, capitalization, and number usage

UNIT

III

PROOFREADING LABELS AND GRAPHICS
(Odd documEnts)

Y ou have seen your ability to proofread business documents
develop as you have completed the previous chapters. You are
now ready to complete the business correspondence component by
reviewing the formatting of envelopes and mailing labels.

The formatting of these items conforms to the guidelines of the U.S.
Postal Service. These guidelines have been developed to
complement the technology currently available for handling and
sorting mail. When you observe these guidelines, you are simply
helping to move your own mail along efficiently and quickly.

Here are your goals for this chapter:

- Review U.S. Postal Service formatting guidelines.
- Improve your ability to punctuate business documents
  correctly.
- Continue to develop your proofreading skill.

PROOFREADING FOR FORMAT

ENVELOPES AND MAILING LABELS

The most popular sizes for envelopes are $4\frac{1}{2}$ inches wide by
$9\frac{1}{2}$ inches long (business or large envelope) and $3\frac{1}{2}$ inches wide by
$6\frac{1}{2}$ inches long (small envelope).

Mailing labels are commonly used for bulk mail. Increasingly they are used on business envelopes. They come in a variety of sizes. The major word processing software packages include a printer selection to facilitate the preparation of labels.

Scanning envelopes and mailing labels involves two steps:

1. Verify that the placement of the address is within the *read zone* of the scanners used in postal sorting facilities.
2. Review the format of the addresses.

The following pages will help you complete each of these steps quickly.

LARGE (BUSINESS) ENVELOPE WITH READ ZONE HIGHLIGHTED

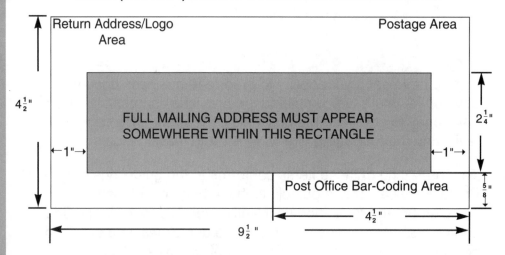

FORMATTING CHECKPOINTS

✔ Be sure the address appears within the read zone.
✔ Check that the format of the address adheres to four principles:
   1. All uppercase characters are used.
   2. No punctuation is used.
   3. Only standard abbreviations are used.
   4. The correct ZIP Code or ZIP+4 Code is always used.
✔ Make sure that the address consists of three or four lines at most and that it is single-spaced.
✔ Check that the desired delivery point appears immediately above the bottom line when a dual address (street address and box number) is used.
✔ Include notations such as CONFIDENTIAL a double space below the return address—never below the mailing address.

✔ Include mailing instructions such as SPECIAL DELIVERY a
   double space below the postage stamp.
✔ Key the return address in the upper left-hand corner, single-
   spaced, about two lines down from the top and three
   spaces in from the left edge if it is not a business envelope
   with a printed return address.
✔ Use the same address guidelines for envelopes in preparing
   and proofing labels.
✔ Center the address on the label.
✔ Affix mailing labels within the read zone. It is very important
   that the label be straight horizontally (scanners cannot
   read a slanted line).
✔ Create a macro for addressing and printing labels. While this
   may require some experimentation on your part, it ensures
   that all of your labels are done in the same way and saves
   proofreading time.

Refer to the Formatting Checkpoints and scan the following
business envelope. Use proofreaders' marks to indicate any
format errors.

```
[RETURN ADDRESS]



REGISTERED     SHADY PINES RESORT

               P.O. BOX 475

               LAKE OF THE WOODS MISSOURI 65201
```

Check your work in the Answer Key at the back of this book.

Read the following short letter, and note the highlighted text. These highlights illustrate common errors in punctuation. Do you understand each error? This section provides a review of major points of punctuation for you.

    Our annual sales seminar begins on Monday, June 29 at 9 a.m. at the Hotel Lowe in Harrisburg, Pennsylvania. Robert Bohannon, M.D. will be the featured speaker. The fee of $50 includes registration, lunch and copies of the proceedings.

    Elections will be held on Tuesday. Nominees are Ruth Simpson, president, Jason Friedman, Secretary, and Nina Rocco, treasurer.

    Don't be disappointed, send in your registration today.

PRINCIPLES AND PRACTICE
PUNCTUATION

There are many rules covering the marks of punctuation—in fact, too many to be cited in one section of a chapter. Also, punctuation practices vary among users as well as among respected authorities. Therefore, the primary purpose of this chapter will be to review those uses of punctuation that contribute to the meaning, clarity, or accuracy of text.

The principles for applying punctuation will be presented within two categories: (1) end or terminal punctuation marks and (2) internal punctuation marks. The principles of internal punctuation will be further subdivided into those that signify pauses, such as commas and semicolons, and those that add clarity to the text, such as parentheses and dashes.

▼ PRINCIPLE 1: Periods

• A period is used to end complete thoughts, including courteous requests and indirect questions (paraphrases of the actual question).

   The graduate student is preparing her thesis.
   Will you please respond by May 15.
   She asked if I was interested in the training.

- Periods are used within initials, academic degrees, and many abbreviations.

E.D. Davison	Sept.
Margaret J. Thompson, Ph.D.	Inc.

- Do not use a period in abbreviated organization names and acronyms.

YWCA	NBC
NATO	WATS

- Use periods after letters or numbers in outlines and lists.

I. Quality Circles	1. Detroit
A. Definition	2. Chicago
B. Implementation	3. Minneapolis

Add or delete periods in the following sentences.

1. Will you respond as quickly as possible to my letter,
2. C.A. Brownson, MD. is our guest lecturer.
3. The stock exchanges are commonly referred to as the N.Y.S.E., the A.M.E.X., and the N.A.S.D.A.Q.
4. I. Primary Computer Printers
   A. Dot-matrix
   B. Letter-quality
   II. Optical Character Readers
5. Leslie asked if our present insurance program was adequate.

> *Check your work in the Answer Key.*
> *Refer to Principle 1 if you had any difficulty.*

▼ PRINCIPLE 2: Question Marks and Exclamation Points

- Use a question mark after a direct question.

  Did you finish your report?

- Use a question mark at the end of a statement that contains a direct question.

  You have ordered the participants' notebooks, haven't you?

- Use an exclamation point to express strong feeling or emotion.

  This is a real surprise!
  I don't believe this happened!

Refer to Principle 2, and add question marks or exclamation points to the following sentences.

1. When will the first draft be ready for review?
2. Congratulations on your promotion!
3. Where is our next seminar scheduled?
4. Tell me: What is the current status of the study?
5. Unbelievable! How else can I describe it?

Check your work in the Answer Key.
Refer to Principle 2 if you had any difficulty.

▼ **PRINCIPLE 3: Commas with Independent Clauses, Series, and Coordinate Adjectives**

- Use a comma to separate two independent clauses joined by a conjunction. (Another way of stating this principle is: The comma is used to separate the parts of a compound sentence.)

  John served as chairperson, and I served as recorder.

  If the clauses are very short, the comma may be omitted.

  I called and Brenda answered.

- Use a comma to separate the items in a series. It is common business practice to use the comma before the conjunction in a series.

  The order included invoices, purchase orders, and expense reports.

  He intended to travel to Omaha to talk with the sales staff, to tour the new offices, and to visit the plant.

- Two adjectives modifying the same noun are called *coordinate adjectives.* Use a comma to separate coordinate adjectives.

    The travel agent specializes in long, restful cruises.

Answering two questions will help you identify coordinate adjectives:

◀ **PROOFREADING POINTER**

- Can the adjectives be transposed?
- Can the word *and* logically be inserted between them?

If the answer to both questions is yes, separate the adjectives with a comma.

Use proofreaders' marks to insert commas in the following sentences.

1. Ralph has proven to be a dedicated, responsible department supervisor.
2. Our group is meeting tomorrow morning, and we will resolve the problem of lower production levels.
3. The agenda includes employee absenteeism, low morale, and negative work attitudes.
4. Send your reply in the stamped, self-addressed envelope.
5. The minutes of the meeting are ready, and they will be distributed tomorrow.

> *Check your work in the Answer Key.*
> *Refer to Principle 3 if you had any difficulty.*

▼ PRINCIPLE 4: Commas with Phrases and Clauses

- Use a comma with interrupting words, phrases, and clauses.

    The LAN, however, has made it possible for us to share the workload.
    She will fly in for the meeting, if necessary.
    When I receive my registration information, I will send in my reservation immediately.

- Omit the comma if the introductory phrase is very short.

    On December 15 we will make a final decision.

- Omit the comma when a dependent clause falls at the end of a sentence.

    I will send in my reservation *when I receive my registration information*.

- Use a comma to set off nonessential modifiers.

    My aunt Ruth, *who lives in Houston*, is a neurosurgeon. We must complete some immediate tasks, *including verifying the names and positions of the respondents and sending thank you letters*, before we can complete the proposal.

- Omit the comma before or after essential modifiers.

    The U.S. Customs House *located in New York* now qualifies for inclusion in the register of National Historical Buildings.
    The technician *who installed the system* is the only one who can answer your question.

- Use a comma to set off words of direct address.

    Professor, should we support the motion?
    You see, *Mr. Martin*, I do intend to complete my work.

▼ **PRINCIPLE 5: Commas with Personal and Company Abbreviations**

- Use commas to set off a person's professional position or educational degree.

    Ricardo Esperanza, C.P.A., was the keynote speaker.
    Roxanne Rodgers, C.L.U., advised the committee on employees' insurance needs.

PROOFREADING POINTER ▶

- There may be times or organizations in which periods are not used when referring to groups of people holding the same title. For example, "We will hire two MBAs." When you are uncertain, the best guideline is to be consistent.

- The trend is to eliminate commas setting off personal and company abbreviations that are part of the name. However, some people and companies still use commas. Follow individual preferences and practices when known.

> Canadian Industries Ltd. is located in Toronto.
> Eldred Barneski Jr. is executive vice-president of our firm.

Use your best judgment in determining whether these sentences need commas. Use proofreaders' marks to insert or delete commas as necessary.

1. Our corporate librarian, Christine Blews, M.L.S., was nominated for an outstanding literary award.
2. After I complete my degree, I intend to apply for the management development program.
3. Am I correct, Cynthia, that you designed this month's newsletter?
4. I will take my vacation when the project is completed.
5. Passing the state bar exam, which is my immediate goal, will enable me to fulfill a lifelong dream.
6. Xydec Inc. will be the major supplier.
7. Sara Greenstein and Lynn Resnick, Jr., have been chosen "Employees of the Month."

> *Check your work in the Answer Key.*
> *Refer to Principles 4 and 5 if you had any difficulty.*

▼ PRINCIPLE 6: Semicolons

With one exception, semicolons always separate parts of compound sentences. In other words, the words that appear on each side of the semicolon can actually be punctuated as two simple sentences.

- Use a semicolon to replace a conjunction in a compound sentence. The following sentence is written two ways to help you understand this.

Compound sentence with a conjunction:

> The tests have been given, and the results have been posted.

Same sentence with a semicolon replacing the conjunction:

> The tests have been given; the results have been posted.

- Use a semicolon when a compound sentence is very long or already contains commas.

    Since Janet is moving to Seattle, she will seek a new position; and she hopes to use her computer knowledge in a position with a major company.

- When one part of a compound sentence contains a comma because of a transitional phrase, use a semicolon to separate the parts.

    Harry did not receive the promotion; therefore, he is seeking a new position.

- When a series already has internal commas, use a semicolon between the parts of the series to enhance readability.

    The new mail clerk has lived in Detroit, Michigan; Akron, Ohio; and Newark, New Jersey.

Use proofreaders' marks to insert semicolons as needed in these sentences.

1. Those present were Roger Babcock, chairperson, Loren Balyeat, secretary, and Diane Faw, controller.
2. We did not purchase the Superior computers, however, we will reconsider the bid for the new division.
3. Ergonomics is an important consideration, a task force has been appointed to prepare a status report on the topic.
4. While we intend to introduce a graphics package soon, we are concentrating on other peripherals, but we will keep you informed on the progress of the proposed software.
5. Teresa McCandless, my immediate supervisor, has asked me to chair the committee, and I have willingly accepted the challenge.

Check your work in the Answer Key.
Refer to Principle 6 if you had any difficulty.

▼ PRINCIPLE 7: Colons, Hyphens, and Dashes

Follow these guidelines when using colons.

- Use a colon to introduce lists and enumerations.

    You will need the following supplies: a textbook, a ruler, and a pocket calculator.

- Use a colon to introduce long quotations.

  The speaker said: "It is to our advantage to study the population decline now. At a later date it will have reached even more disastrous levels from an employment standpoint."

Hyphens have two uses.

- Hyphens are used to join *compound adjectives*—two adjectives forming one idea—before a noun.

  He ordered several lengths of 6-inch copper tubing. They certainly did a first-class job.

- Hyphens are used in a series of compound adjectives modifying the same noun.

  The child excelled on the first-, second-, and third-grade tests.

Follow these guidelines for using dashes.

- Use a dash to indicate an abrupt break in thought or to add an afterthought. Careful writers use dashes sparingly.

  We will not be participating this year—as you might have already guessed.

- On some keyboards, a dash is formed by keying two hyphens. Newer word processing and desktop publishing programs allow you to create a solid dash (called the *em dash*). These programs also allow you to key an *en dash* to indicate a range, such as 1890–1950.

PROOFREADING POINTER

Use proofreaders' marks to add colons, hyphens, and dashes to the following paragraph.

```
    The fifth-floor supervisor suggested that the
following issues be included in the discussion
relocation of all furniture, purchase of new
furniture, or a combination of the two her particular
preference. For your information, the idea of making
the move on Saturday was rejected by a two thirds
vote of those involved.
```

Check your work in the Answer Key.
Refer to Principle 7 if you had any difficulty.

MASTERY CHECKPOINT ONE

Use proofreaders' marks to add or delete the appropriate end marks of punctuation in the following short paragraphs.

1. Will you please mark July 10 on your calendar now? That is the date we have chosen for our company picnic We are looking for volunteers for three committees:

   1 Promotion
   2 Entertainment
   3 Food and Beverages

2. I can't believe you did that Didn't you think of the long term effects of your recent action That could have serious consequences for your future in the organization don't you think Marissa asked if you could meet in her office at 9 a.m. tomorrow to discuss the situation

Check your work in the Answer Key.
Review Principles 1 and 2 if you had any difficulty.

MASTERY CHECKPOINT TWO

Proof the following paragraphs from business letters for punctuation errors. Use proofreaders' marks to add or delete punctuation as needed.

1. It is our intent to study the following areas, human resources, finance and long range planning. When the study is completed the task-force will prepare a comprehensive up to date summary.

2. On the new system you can access online libraries, newspapers, encyclopedias, bulletin boards, banking services and more, these will all be at your fingertips. This is an exciting development.

Check your work in the Answer Key.

Study Table 7-1 to review the formatting of marks of punctuation. Refer to it as needed as you continue to develop your proofreading skill.

Table 7-1. Punctuation Marks

FORMATTING OF MARKS OF PUNCTUATION			
Mark of Punctuation	**Usage in Text**	**Spaces**	**Placement with Quotation Marks**
Period	End of sentence Enumerations and listings End of abbreviations Within abbreviations End of sentence in desktop publishing applications using proportional font	2 2 1 0 1	Always precedes
Question mark	End of sentence	2	Precedes when quoted material is a question; follows when lead-in clause is the question
Exclamation point	End of sentence	2	Same as question
Comma		1	Always precedes
Semicolon		1	Always follows
Colon		2	Always follows
Hyphen	Within text	0	
Dash	Within text	0	

PERFORMANCE CHALLENGE

PROOFREADING ENVELOPES AND MAILING LABELS

The proofreading emphasis in this unit is on business materials that are noncontinuous text. The content and format are quite different from those you have been working with. Numbers and abbreviations may be a part of the materials you will use. This unusual text requires a different proofreading approach.

Proofreading documents with special formats such as envelopes and mailing labels:

1. Scan the envelope or label first. Is the address placed within the read zone? Is it keyed in all caps with no punctuation?
2. Slow down and proofread on a character-by-character basis when proofreading noncontinuous text. There is no sense of continuity to help you. Each word or numeral stands on its own. You will find it very helpful to vocalize (read aloud very quietly) this type of copy as you proofread.

3. Compare each part of the mailing address to the letter or document that accompanies it.
4. Be certain that the ZIP Code is correct—this is the most important item for processing your mail.

Proof the following envelope addresses for correct format. Review the Formatting Checkpoints. Use proofreaders' marks to indicate errors.

```
                    KIM CHANG
                    YEIKO SCIENTIFIC INSTRUMENTS
                    PO BOX 3456
                    SAN JOSE CA   95101-3345

          Confidential
```

```
                    Dr. Gwynn Melrose
                    7765 Magnum Pass
                    Torrance, CA   90503
```

```
                    CITIZEN MUTUAL INSURANCE GROUP
                    420 LEXINGTON AVENUE
                    NEW YORK NEW YORK   1170
```

Check your work in the Answer Key.

Document 1: Scan the addresses on the mailing labels below. Refer to the format on page 119, as necessary. Use proofreaders' marks to indicate errors.

```
BLENHEIM, LTD.

PO BOX 1020

SANTA MONICA CA   90404-1020
```

```
EVERETT SAVINGS BANK
410 NEW CIRCLE ROAD
LOUISVILLE KENTUCKY   40225
```

```
North Irvine Training Center
2323 Fourth Avenue
Laurel, Md.   20708
```

```
B. H. Johnstone
Breckenridge Hotel
Corner of Main and Locust Streets
P. O. Box 1001
Columbus, OH   43215
```

Document 2: Proofread the following paragraphs for errors in punctuation. Use proofreaders' marks to indicate errors.

Computers are everywhere today-at home, at the office, at your bank, at your travel agent and in your schools. In fact who would think of running a business without one. But does the ubiquitous nature of computers guarantee that we are more productive? Is our amount of work up, and our efficiency down? Or has our level of efficiency risen with the increased amount of work we are producing?

Part of the answer lies in the system and software we have available. Most computer representatives today recommend no less than an 80386 based system, an 80486 is preferable, and the 80586s are just around the corner for many of us. We need 4 to 8 M.B. of memory on the system, and 8 to 15 MB of hard disk storage.

The software you select should correspond to the type of documents you prepare. High end word processors may include such sophisticated features as drawing and charting functions; multicolumn pages; indexing; and table of contents. A less sophisticated package will meet your needs, if the bulk of your work is letters and simple reports.

The infamous "bottom line" is There is a system just for you.

Document 3: Proofread the following two documents for any errors in format or language. Use proofreaders' marks to indicate errors.

```
                                              ☐

          J.C. BURNSTEIN
          887 ROXBURY LANE
          BINGHAMTON NEW YORK 13961
```

```
May 15, 19XX


Janice C. Bernstein
8878 Roxbury Lane
Binghamton, NY  13916

Dear Customer:

Thank you for your letter of May 9, 19XX, regarding the
unavailability of merchandise in our spring catalog.  You
are correct--each of the three items you ordered were, in
fact, out of stock.

Unfortunately thats not all the bad news.  The largest item
in your order, the Puls-a-matic blender, has been recalled
and we cannot give you any additional information on it or
on a possible replacement for it.  Now for the good news:
the Dirt Quick sweeper and the Debonair crystal set are in
stock, and are being shipped to you today.

You have been a good customer; and we want to keep you.  I
am enclosing a $25 gift certificate to be used on the
merchandize of your choice.  If you encounter any similiar
difficulties on future orders, would you please call me on
my direct line: 1-800-775-5252?  Thanks for taking the time
to write.

                    Sincerely



                    Lurinda Beecham
                    Customer Service Supervisor

xxx
```

PROOFREADING ALERT

Some words have more than one correct spelling, such as *catalog/catalogue, adviser/advisor, traveled/travelled,* and *programmed/programed.* Be consistent in your usage.

Document 4: Proof this draft copy of a new claim form to be used in your office.

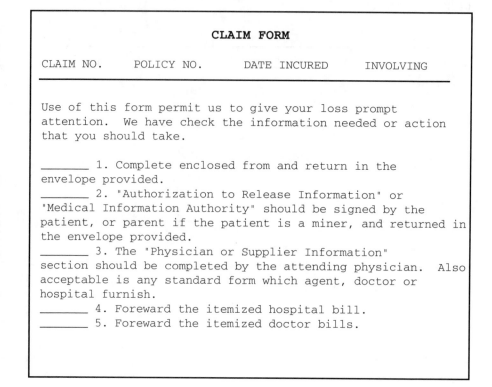

CLAIM FORM

CLAIM NO.   POLICY NO.   DATE INCURED   INVOLVING

Use of this form permit us to give your loss prompt attention. We have check the information needed or action that you should take.

_____ 1. Complete enclosed from and return in the envelope provided.
_____ 2. "Authorization to Release Information" or "Medical Information Authority" should be signed by the patient, or parent if the patient is a miner, and returned in the envelope provided.
_____ 3. The "Physician or Supplier Information" section should be completed by the attending physician. Also acceptable is any standard form which agent, doctor or hospital furnish.
_____ 4. Foreward the itemized hospital bill.
_____ 5. Foreward the itemized doctor bills.

In Chapter 7 you developed your proofreading skill on documents with special formats—envelopes and labels. This chapter will enable you to continue to build a mastery level skill on another item with noncontinuous text—tables.

Tables are an integral part of many business reports. Tables enhance the text of a report by presenting information in graphic form and providing more information in less space. The ability to format tables to maximize readability is a critical skill for today's business employee.

Here are your goals for this chapter:

- Review the formatting of three types of tables, commonly referred to as open, ruled, and boxed.
- Review your knowledge of capitalization principles and practices.
- Further enhance your proofreading skill.

PROOFREADING FOR FORMAT

TABLES

As you review the format of a table, there are three terms you will need to know: *column, row*, and *cell*.

- A column presents information vertically (generally top to bottom).
- A row presents information horizontally (generally left to right).
- A cell is the juncture between a column and a row.

These parts are labeled in the table on page 138.

Three types of tables are commonly used in business documents: *open, ruled*, and *boxed*.

- An open table contains no rules (lines).
- A ruled table uses horizontal rules.
- A boxed table uses both horizontal and vertical rules.

Each of these is illustrated on the pages that follow.

Note: The boxed table has grown in popularity because of the ease with which it can be created in word processing. You should master this very versatile feature of your software if you have not already done so.

OPEN TABLE

```
                   JOB TITLES FOR WORD PROCESSING

                           January 19XX


        Employer                        Job Title

    Western Imports          Word Processing Specialist

    A-One Advertising        Communications Specialist

    Western Utilities        Correspondence Secretary

    Fantasy Travel           Communications Technician
```

✔ The open table has no rules.
✔ It is positioned to appear centered horizontally.
✔ The title of the table is centered in all caps. You may omit the titles of tables within memos if the lead-in is adequately descriptive of the information.
✔ The column heads are centered; they may also be flush left.
✔ The text in the body of the table may be either single- or double-spaced.

RULED TABLE

```
              CIRCULATION SUMMARY
_____
        Three Years Ending December 1993
_____

Region    Manager      1991      1992      1993

North     J. Ryan      35,330    34,290    35,750
South     M. Peete     29,338    30,229    31,103
East      K. Wells     32,890    33,340    35,014
West      P. Kitts     36,110    36,895    36,451
_____
```

✔ The ruled table has horizontal lines. The placement of these may vary, but they are generally as shown here: before and after the subheading, or before and after the column heads; after the last line of the body.

✔ The title is centered in all caps.

✔ The column heads are flush left with initial caps for major words. These heads also can be centered.

✔ The information in the rows is flush left. Columns containing decimals are aligned at the decimal.

✔ Note that the spacing between columns is not even. In this example, the text columns are spaced to show their relationship; there is more space between the second text column and the first numeric column; the numeric columns are spaced to show their relationship. Spacing such as that shown enhances the readability of the table.

BOXED TABLE

ODYSSEY ELECTRONICS			
Administrative Assistants			
Employee Name	Soc. Sec. No.	Date of Birth	Date of Hire
M.J. Kimmeroth	379-90-7865	7-17-54	3-14-94
Maria Montez	286-30-7656	9-30-65	6-19-94
Lee Epstein	330-78-7642	3-15-68	8-17-95
Brenda Windsor	345-90-8897	6-12-63	5-5-94

Row →

Cell ——→   Column ——→

FORMATTING CHECKPOINTS

✔ The formatting of the title and subtitle are the same as in open and ruled tables.

✔ The column heads are centered. (In some cases these may be flush left, but they must be formatted consistently.)

✔ The cell information is centered. (This text may also be flush left, but it must be formatted consistently.)

✔ The table is centered horizontally on the page.

FORMATTING CHECKPOINTS FOR ALL TABLES

✔ Create a name for the table that is descriptive of the information presented. Key the title in all caps.

✔ Use short, clear headings for columns and rows. Capitalize all major words.

✔ Be consistent in your placement of titles. Column heads may be flush left or centered. Row headings are generally flush left.

✔ Format information within cells consistently flush left, centered, or decimal aligned.

✔ If the table contains lengthy portions of text or information, use additional spacing to separate logical groups.

✔ If a document has several tables or figures, assign each a number. Include a list of tables and/or figures as part of the front matter.

✔ Center tables appearing within text. Wide tables may extend to the margins.

✔ Center tables that appear alone on a page.

Refer to the Formatting Checkpoints and scan the following ruled table. Use proofreaders' marks to indicate any format errors.

```
                      Courses and Professors
_____

                       Winter Term, 19XX

Course                                  Professor
_____

Business Communication          Dr. Missling
Economics 111                   Dr. Ellickson
Advanced Keyboarding            Professor Johnson
Physical Education              Dr. Wigglesworth
Accounting                      Dr. Ozello
Psychology                      Professor Manning
Statistics                      Professor Graine
```

Check your work in the Answer Key at the back of this book.

USING LANGUAGE EFFECTIVELY

CAPITALIZATION

Proof the short memo below, and note the bold text. The highlighted type illustrates common errors in capitalization. Do you understand each error? This section provides a review of major principles and practices in capitalization.

```
MEMORANDUM

TO:       Marketing Staff
FROM:     P. E. Richards
DATE:     August 1, 19XX
SUBJECT: Extended Holiday Leave

Daniel Bostwick, Director Of Human Resources, has informed
me that the following policy will be in effect for
Extended Holiday Leave over the Labor day weekend,
September 3-6, 19XX.

POLICY CLARIFICATION (see section IIIa-b, page 143, of the
PERQ master labor agreement):

Requests for Extended Leave (or vacation days) during the
week preceding or following Labor Day must be submitted in
writing to one of the Employment Compensation Specialists
no later than August 10.

The Director reminds us that the week prior to Labor Day
is a very slow time; the reduced charge is used as an
incentive to encourage vacation time prior to the Fall,
our busiest season.
```

PROOFREADING ALERT

Except for periods that follow abbreviations and apostrophes, all punctuation marks must follow parentheses.

Capitalization is one of the earliest language skills you learned. Capitalizing the first words of sentences and proper nouns is done virtually without thinking. There are other capitalization practices, however, that send many of us to a reference source.

In addition to general principles of capitalization, there are capitalization practices that are unique to a company or organization. As an employee, you must combine those principles and practices in a consistent and satisfactory way. Consistency is the key word.

When proofreading copy for capitalization errors, it is necessary to distinguish between initial caps as in Betty Clark and all caps as in TIME. You may assume throughout this chapter that capitalization refers to initial caps only. All caps will be specifically stated where it is applicable.

▼ PRINCIPLE 1: First Words

The capitalization of the first word of a sentence does not need to be reviewed. However, there are other "first word" capitalization principles that you will find helpful.

- Capitalize the first word of a full-sentence quotation.

   The president made the surprising announcement, "We have purchased a controlling interest in D & J Industries."

- Capitalize the first word after a colon only when a complete sentence follows.

   The rule is: No employee may request personal leave on the day immediately preceding or following a scheduled holiday.

- Capitalize the first word in listed items when the items are designated by letters, numbers, or other symbols.

   1. The minutes of the July meeting
   2. The agenda for the August meeting
   3. Copies of handouts for the August meeting

- Capitalize the first words in sections of formal outlines.

  I. Introduction
  II. Project history
      A. Precorporate involvement
      B. Initial proposal
      C. Implementation problems

- Capitalize each major word in a salutation but only the first word in a closing.

  Salutation: Dear Personnel Director:
  Closing: Sincerely yours,

Use proofreaders' marks to add capitals to the following paragraph.

```
    the article began:  "the only decision more difficult
than choosing a computer is selecting the right
printer." you may choose from two types:  impact and
nonimpact. your final decision should be based on
your needs.
```

Check your work in the Answer Key.
Review Principle 1 if you had any difficulty.

▼ **PRINCIPLE 2: Proper Nouns**

Common nouns name classes or groups of people, places, and things. *Proper nouns* refer to specific people, places, or things. Proper adjectives are derived from proper nouns.

- Capitalize proper nouns and proper adjectives.

Common nouns	Proper nouns	Proper adjectives
president	Andrew Jackson	the Jackson years
university	Harvard University	a Harvard graduate
prince	Prince Edward II	the Edwardian age

- Capitalize only those parts of hyphenated terms that are proper nouns or adjectives.

  the French-speaking world   President-elect Hayes

- Capitalize geographical place names and regions.

    Dallas   the city of Ames   Mount Everest

- Capitalize alternative names for geographical places.

    the Windy City   the Sun Belt   the Big Apple

- Capitalize the names of directions only when they refer to actual regions or a person from that region.

    the Southwest   a Southerner   West Coast
    just east of here   southern Florida

- Capitalize days of the week, months, and holidays.

    Monday, September 5   Yom Kippur
    Veterans' Day   New Year's Day

- Capitalize words that precede or are designated by numbers when they represent complete titles or labels. Do not capitalize partial or common labels.

Complete titles	**Common/partial titles**
Typewriting II	business courses
Room 816	second floor rooms
Invoice 84573	this month's invoices

Use proofreaders' marks to add or delete capitals to the following short paragraph.

> Our new satellite office, located on the East side
> of Exeter Boulevard in the great Southwest city of
> Santa Fe, New Mexico, is having its Grand Opening on
> April 23, 19XX. Mark Ewing, Professor of Endocrinology
> and President-Elect of the local University faculty
> group, will give the keynote address. Platform guests
> should meet in the second floor Conference Room at
> 1:30 p.m.

Check your work in the Answer Key.
Review Principle 2 if you had any difficulty.

▼ PRINCIPLE 3: Titles

The capitalization of titles varies widely. Be certain you follow any practices or preferences of your employer and that you are consistent in your capitalization.

- Capitalize titles that precede or are part of a person's name.

  President David McKenna   Sister Mary Angeline
  Councilwoman Joan Deigan   Queen Elizabeth

- Do not capitalize a title if the name is set off by commas.

  our president, Yvonne Reinhold

- Generally do not capitalize occupational or other titles such as *manager, consultant, mother*, or *grandfather*.

- Capitalize a title when used in direct address.

  Did I hear you correctly, Professor?

- Capitalize the names of committees and departments when they are the official names.

  Our Financial Services Department is expanding its space.
  but
  Our research department is behind schedule. (The official name is Research and Development Department.)

- Capitalize major words in names of government bodies and official organizations.

  the Reagan Administration   the University of Miami
  the First Baptist Church   the Internal Revenue Service

- Capitalize all major words in titles of written or performed works.

  "How to Computerize a Small Business"
  The American Heritage Dictionary (*The* is part of the title)

- Capitalize brand names but not the products themselves.

  IBM computer   Centel telephone
  WordPerfect software

▼ **PRINCIPLE 4: Subject Lines and Headings**

The formatting of subject lines and headings assumes many appearances: initial caps, all caps, underlining, and, increasingly, italics.

- The subject line of memos may appear in all caps or initial caps. Some writers also boldface the subject to make reading and filing easier.

SUBJECT: <u>Opening of New Office</u>

- Underlining may be used very effectively with initial caps. However, do not underline all-caps or boldface copy.

SUBJECT: OPENING OF NEW OFFICE
SUBJECT: **OPENING OF NEW OFFICE**

- Side headings in reports may appear in all caps or with initial caps (underlining optional). Side headings should be formatted consistently throughout the report.

Section 1: Discussion of the Problem
THE FUTURE OF THE WIDGET
<u>Networking Systems</u>

- Book titles may be typed in italics or underscored.

<u>Successful Business Dress</u> or *Successful Business Dress*

Use proofreaders' marks to add or delete capital letters in the following paragraph.

    We found the chapter "A Positive Approach To
Conflict Management" in Author Tustin's new book,
<u>SUCCESSFUL NEGOTIATIONS</u>, very helpful in resolving
the differences between the Accounting and Corporate
Audit departments. Joanna Glancy and Norton Holmes,
the respective Department Managers, applied the
Author's approach to their situation and are very
happy with the results.

Check your work in the Answer Key.
Review Principles 3 and 4 if you had any difficulty.

> Use proofreaders' marks to add or delete the appropriate capitals in the following short paragraphs.

MASTERY CHECKPOINT ONE

1. The chairman of the board announced: "we are very pleased to announce the acquisition of the following properties:

   1. the Southwest corner of Phoenix and Grand Streets
   2. a 2-acre plot just East of our present site on Ramada Avenue
   3. the former home of Senator-Elect Murphy"

2. The renovation of the Third Floor Employee Cafeteria has begun. The details of funding for this project are in the August Minutes of the OOC.

> *Check your work in the Answer Key.*
> *Review Principles 1 and 2 if you had any difficulty.*

> Use proofreaders' marks to add or delete the appropriate capitals in the following short paragraphs.

MASTERY CHECKPOINT TWO

1. The community group in the City was very eager to hear the newly elected Mayor present his plan for neighborhood renewal. These people are a dynamic group of activists; Mayor Laverty pledged the full support of his Administration to their efforts.

2. Brian Gimbel, author of YOU CAN MAKE A DIFFERENCE!, had the group on the edge of their seats. As a former Director within the U.S. Department of Justice and Chairman of Employee Relations, he certainly has the background to understand today's business environment.

> *Check your work in the Answer Key.*
> *Review Principles 3 and 4 if you had any difficulty.*

This section gives you another opportunity to develop your proofreading skill with noncontinuous text. As in Chapter 7, your primary proofreading techniques will be to slow down and, where appropriate, read on a character-by-character basis.

Proofreading documents with tables:

1. Scan the table. Do you like its appearance? Is it centered on the page? Does it appear readable? Does it seem to be clear in its presentation?
2. Are related columns and rows, as well as cells, formatted consistently?
3. Is the style of details, such as abbreviations, numbers, and symbols, consistent?
4. Is the information in numeric columns aligned?
5. If technical terms are used, proofread them each time they appear.

Document 1: Proofread the following boxed table for correct and consistent format. Review the Formatting Checkpoints for boxed tables. Use proofreaders' marks to indicate errors.

TEMPORARY OFFICE SUPPORT STAFF		
Reasons why businesses use Temporary Help*		
Reasons	Frequent Users	Occasional Users
Peak Load Periods	86.5%	
Temporary Replacement	48.6%	46.7%
Vacation Replacement	70.3%	40.5%
One-time Projects	54.1%	40.0%
Specialized work	27.0	13.5%
Potential Hire	18.9%	8.4%
Lower Employee Cost	10.8%	3.4%
Less Paperwork	2.7%	1.7%

*The Office, August 1986

Document 2: Scan the open table below. Refer to the format on page 136, as necessary. Use proofreaders' marks to indicate errors.

```
                    Estimated Expenses
                      May, 19XX

Postage                        $ 2,035
Software                         1,900
Telephone                      $12,960
Office Supplies                             600
Copier                             600
Depreciation                     8,560

Secretarial help               14,900

Total                          $38,655
```

Document 3: Proofread the following page from a multipage report for errors in spelling and capitalization. Use proofreaders' marks to indicate errors.

```
    It is projected that the system will be installed
in a four-phase Implementation Plan.  These are
detailed below.

Phase I

Phase I will be implemented immediately.  Charles
Rivers, Systems Supervisor, will direct the
implementation. It will include a central Primus
Computer for handling the loan system at the
Administrative Offices in Bloomington. The system
must meet the following requirements for work
stations:

WORK STATION SITE    Initial Number    Maximum Number

Marketing                 1                   2
Production                1                   4
Operations                0                   4
G & A                     2                   8
Data processing           1                   2
Computer bank             1                   2

Each work station must have at least one Quik-Print
Laser Printer.
```

• The table in Document 3 is an example of a table without a major title. The lead-in sentence introduces the information that follows.

PROOFREADING
POINTER

Document 4a: You received the following note from your supervisor, Johanna Brigitte. Since you were involved in a top-priority project, you asked an intern to type the memo. The document he keyed is the second one shown, Document 4b.

```
From the desk of...

          Johanna Brigitte


Please send a memo to Lorraine Medico in International
Relations providing her with the information from our
reference materials that she requested.  Be sure to let her
know we are happy to be of assistance at any time.

INTERNATIONAL SOURCES OF REFERENCE MATERIALS

Algeria      Oran          COMMISSARIAT NATIONAL AU
                           RECENSEMENT DE LA POPULATION

Chile        Santiago      INSTITUTO NACIONAL DE ESTADISTICOS

France       Paris         INSTITUTE NATIONAL DE LA
                           STATISTIQUE ET DES ETUDES
                           ECONOMIQUES

Mexico       Mexico, D.F.  DIRECCION GENERALO DE ESTADISTRIA

Togo         Lome          DIRECTION DE LA STATISTIQUE

Panama       Panama        DIRECCION DE ESTADISTRIA Y CENSO
```

Document 4b: Proofread the second document against the first. Mark any errors you find.

```
MEMORANDUM


To:  Loraine Medico, International Relations

From:  Johanna Brigitte

Subject:  REFERENCE SOURCES

Date:  September 4, 19XX


The information you requested from our reference
sources are as follows:

      INTERNATIONAL SOURCES OF REFERENCE MATERIAL

Country  City         Reference Source

Algeria  Oran         COMMISSARIAT NATIONAL AU
                      RECENSEMENT DE LA POPULATION

Chile    Santaigo     INSTITUTO NACIONAL DE
                      ESTADISTICOES

France   Paris        INSTITUTE NATIONAL DE LA
                      STATISTIQUE ET DES ETUDE
                      ECONOMIQUES

Mexico   Mexico, D.F. DIRECCTION GENERALO DE
                      ESTADISTRIA

Togo     Loma         DIRECTION DE LA STATISTIQUES

Panama   Panama       DIRECCION DE ESTADISTRA Y CENSO

Our International relations staff is eager to assist
you at any time.  Please call us.

meg
```

Document 5: Proofread the following memorandum for any errors in language or format. Use proofreaders' marks to indicate errors.

MEMORANDUM

TO: All Sales Representatives

FROM: Richard Veskovitch

DATE: April 15, 19XX

SUBJECT: Sales QUOTAS

Please submit your semiannual Sales Reports to our home office (2100 Executive Plaza, Atlanta, Georgia 30301) as soon as possible. If you wish, you may use the Wats lines to submit your report orally and then follow with a printed copy within a few days.

Planning Conference

Our annual sales planning conference is scheduled for the Hotel Bayside, San Diego, Calif. 92115 on July 5-10. Mark your calendars now.

TRAINING MATERIALS

Three trainers in our Training Area have just published an excellent book titled Yes, You Can Sell! If you have not received your copy, please call my office and request one.

cvc

PROOFREADING ALERT

State names in continuous text are usually spelled out. The two-letter abbreviation is typically used in addresses and similar materials. The two-letter abbreviation has no periods, and both letters are capitalized. Make sure that state names are written the same way in the same situations.

Recent software releases have made adding graphics, or visuals, to business reports a relatively easy task. Graphics include various forms of graphs, which present numeric information in a visual format: organization charts, diagrams, and tables. Graphics greatly enhance the readability of a document. Graphics are powerful, combining communication with visual appeal.

It is important that you, as a proofreader, acquire knowledge of the appropriate use of graphics and develop an ability to interpret graphics to be sure they accurately reflect the information they represent. This chapter will help you feel confident that you can do just that.

Here are your goals for this chapter:

- Proofread visuals for accuracy of presentation.
- Review the use of numbers in business documents.
- Develop your proofreading skill to a mastery level.

PROOFREADING FOR FORMAT
GRAPHICS

Your study of formatting will take on a different twist in this chapter. While you will review formats, you will also interpret information. The proofreader usually does not determine whether a graphic is needed or what type of graphic is appropriate. The proofreader's major task is to proof the information for accuracy. Increasing your understanding of visuals will help you do that.

As with tables, there are some terms you should be familiar with: *unit of measurement, y* or *vertical axis, x* or *horizontal axis*, and *legend*. Each of these is illustrated on the following graph.

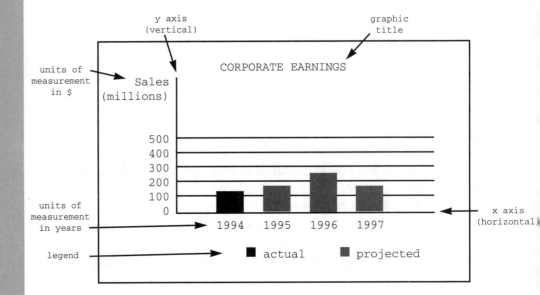

There are four common types of graphs, or charts: *bar, pie, line,* and *organizational charts*. Each is used for a specific purpose.

- Bar charts are used to make comparisons.

- Pie charts illustrate parts-to-whole relationships.

- Line charts illustrate trends.

- Organization charts show the vertical and horizontal relationships within a company or organization. Accuracy is a "must." Names and titles cannot be misspelled.

BAR CHARTS

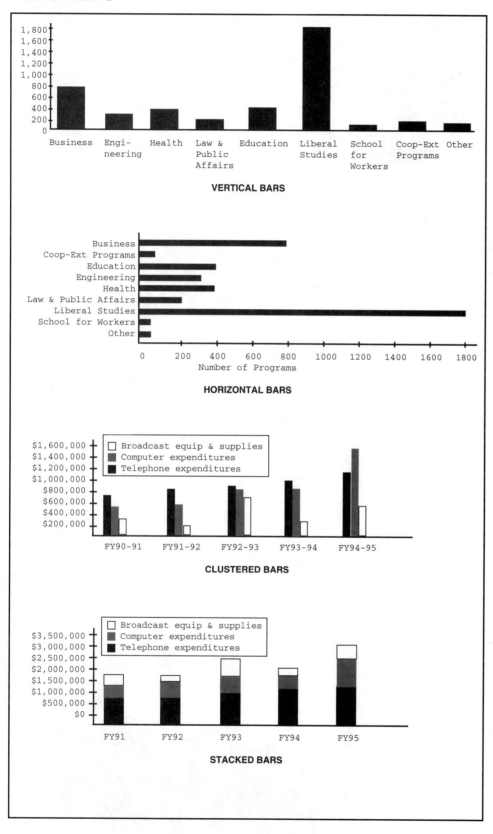

PIE CHART

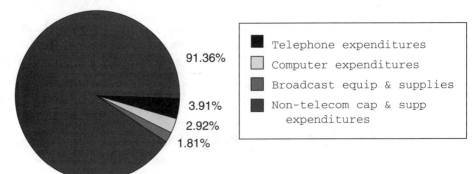

- Telephone expenditures — 91.36%
- Computer expenditures — 3.91%
- Broadcast equip & supplies — 2.92%
- Non-telecom cap & supp expenditures — 1.81%

LINE CHARTS

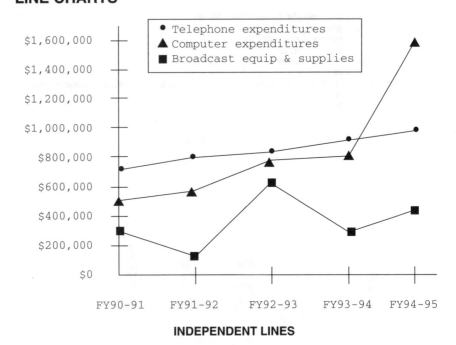

- Telephone expenditures
- Computer expenditures
- Broadcast equip & supplies

INDEPENDENT LINES

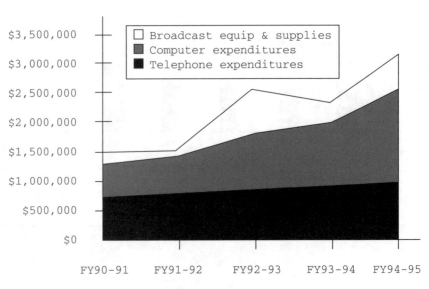

- Broadcast equip & supplies
- Computer expenditures
- Telephone expenditures

STACKED LINES

ORGANIZATION CHART

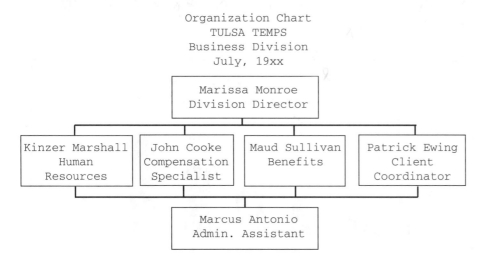

✔ The visual should be placed next to the information it illustrates whenever possible.

✔ Visuals requiring one-fourth page or less are usually placed within the text. Larger visuals are placed on separate pages, positioned on the page immediately following the first reference.

• This suggested placement is offered as a guideline only. The skilled desktop publisher can often arrange the page very attractively to accommodate a larger graphic.

◀ **PROOFREADING POINTER**

✔ Visuals may be placed in appendixes when they represent backup or supplementary information.

✔ Check the clarity of the labels on the graphics. Does the reader have to spend time interpreting the graphic itself first, or does its clarity enable that person to immediately grasp the concept?

✔ Titles are keyed in all caps.

✔ The information on charts should be limited to important items only. If necessary, combine smaller or less important bits of information.

Refer to the appropriate Formatting Checkpoints, and scan the following bar chart. Use proofreaders' marks to indicate any format errors.

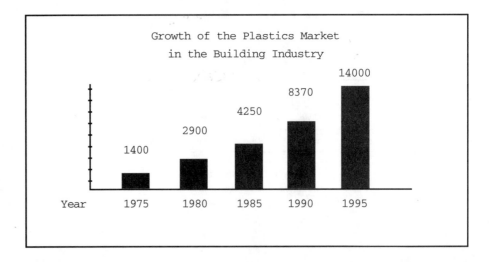

Check your work in the Answer Key at the back of this book.

USING LANGUAGE EFFECTIVELY

NUMBERS

Proof the following paragraphs, and note the highlighted text. These highlights illustrate common errors in the use of numbers in business text. Do you understand each error? This section provides a review of major principles and practices in number usage.

> At least **six** percent of U.S. citizens have traveled to the British Isles within the past year. Even the average temperature of 60 **degrees** does not deter travelers.
>
> The average cost of such a trip is **$2,500.00**. That total represents the following items: airfare, **$950**; lodging, **$750**; car rental, $175.50; meals, $424.50; incidentals, **$200**. The average distance traveled in Great Britain is **seven hundred** miles.
>
> Thirty-five percent of the travelers report that Chapter **Five** of the book, AFFORDABLE TRAVEL, was their guide. While U.S. currency is not commonly used, one traveler reported that she had actually received **73¢** in U.S. coins at a souvenir shop.

Many of the numbers that you use in business may be expressed in figures or in words. It is often a matter of personal choice or corporate practice. Authorities vary in their application of number expression rules.

This chapter is not intended to be a comprehensive guide to writing numbers. Rather, only the most generally accepted guidelines are presented in this chapter, and many of those have acceptable exceptions. The most important guide is consistency and accuracy.

Generally speaking, in business correspondence numbers are written more frequently in words than in figures. On the other hand, numbers are usually expressed in figures in technical material and reports. Whenever you are in doubt as to the most commonly used form, refer to the guidelines in this chapter for assistance.

Throughout this chapter, you will practice your skill in applying consistency to number expressions and verifying their accuracy.

PRINCIPLES AND PRACTICE
NUMBERS

Four major principles affect number usage.

▼ PRINCIPLE 1: Figures or Words?

Authorities tend to agree on two rules for expressing numbers in business correspondence:

- Numbers one through ten are spelled out; numbers over ten are written as figures.

   The department will add *three* new employees.
   The purchase order listed *15* different items.

   Related numbers should be consistent. If related items contain figures above and below ten, the usual practice is to list all items in figures.

   The total order included *15* computers, *5* printers, and *1* plotter.

- The proofreaders' marks you have learned are also used when correcting number copy. Thus 8 would indicate that the figure should be spelled out. Likewise, "We have fifteen available colors" indicates that figures are to be used.   15

PROOFREADING POINTER

Use proofreaders' marks to correct the numbers in the following sentences.

1. We have only 8 sample items left.
2. Margaret gained twenty-five new customers last month.
3. Please repaint all 10 doors.
4. You should have shipped 37 dictionaries, nine word books, and 3 thesauruses.
5. I have one check but 12 deposit slips remaining.

Check your work in the Answer Key.
Review Principle 1 if you had any difficulty.

▼ PRINCIPLE 2: Numbers Expressed as Words

There are some instances of numbers that are almost always spelled out.

- <u>Numbers beginning a sentence</u>. These should always be spelled out. If the number is large, it is a good practice to rearrange the sentence.

  Two students earned meritorious academic status.
  One thousand three hundred twenty students will graduate on Sunday.

  This may be rewritten to read:

  On Sunday *1,320* students will graduate.

- <u>Addresses</u>. Numbered street names one through ten are spelled out. A house or building address of *One* is spelled out.

  Your interview will be held at *4500* Seventh Avenue.
  Their new office address is *One* Wall Street.

- <u>Two numbers appearing together</u>. When two related numbers appear together, generally spell out the smaller one.

  Our new director ordered *37 ten*-pound cartons.

  Note: Some authorities write out the shorter number. Be consistent in usage regardless of which guideline you adopt.

If two unrelated numbers appear together, separate them by a comma.

> By the year *2000, 7,350,000* Americans will be over the age of 65.

- <u>Fractions standing alone</u>. Fractions standing alone within text are spelled out.

> We sold *one-half* of our inventory.

The following paragraph contains several numbers. Use proofreaders' marks to correct any that are expressed in a form not consistent with Principle 2.

```
    67 sales representatives have already confirmed
their plans to attend the annual sales conference to be
held at our corporate headquarters, 1 Fifth Avenue, New
York City. We expect a total attendance of 200, which is
three-fourths of our staff.  We have already reserved
210 2-room suites at the prestigious Hotel Barclay.
```

Check your work in the Answer Key.
Review Principle 2 if you had any difficulty.

▼ PRINCIPLE 3: Numbers Expressed as Figures

The following general guidelines may be observed for expressing numbers in figures.

- <u>Amounts of money</u>. Sums of money are always written in figures.

> $10   59 cents $645.67

Amounts of money less than one dollar are written in figures followed by *cents*. Even dollar amounts are not followed by a decimal and zeros unless other related items include cents.

> The price progression was $5.00, $6.15, and $7.30.

Note: The practice for using the dollar sign varies greatly. It may be repeated before each number, be added only to the first number in a series, or may not appear at all if it is clear from the context that dollar amounts are involved. Your choice should be based on clarity and consistency.

- <u>Measurements and other specifications</u>. Numbers used as measurements, sizes, temperatures, dimensions, and identification always appear in figures.

72°	1,200 miles	129 pounds
5'6"	S.S. #379-03-5615	0.456 centimeters

- <u>Percentages</u>. In business correspondence, the amount of a percentage is stated in figures followed by the word *percent*.

  12 percent   3.5 percent

PROOFREADING POINTER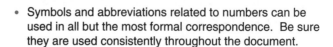

- Symbols and abbreviations related to numbers can be used in all but the most formal correspondence. Be sure they are used consistently throughout the document.

- <u>Numbers following nouns</u>. When a number follows a descriptor such as *Chapter*, *Volume*, *Room*, *Model*, or *page*, it is expressed in figures.

Chapter 9	Policy #120734
Suite 120	page 45

- <u>Numbers in compound adjectives</u>. Numbers in compound adjectives appear in figures.

  20-year mortgage   20-lb. bond paper

Use proofreaders' marks to indicate the correct usage of numbers in the following sentences.

1. The deposit included three items: $50, currency; $12.50, coins; and $75, checks.
2. Since our warehouse space is limited, please ship fifty thirty- lb. bags.
3. Is the middle number of your social security number thirty-one or thirteen?
4. Our new address is Suite Fifteen in the new Pueblo Medical Center.
5. The progressive rates are 3%, 4%, and 4.75 percent.

Check your work in the Answer Key.
Review Principle 3 if you had any difficulty.

▼ PRINCIPLE 4: Numbers in Dates and Times

Use of numbers in dates and times may be guided by the following:

- Dates. The date is always written in figures when it follows the month.

    The new office opened November *14*, 1986.

    Dates expressed as ordinal numbers (5th or fifth) are *only* used when the day precedes the month.

    We will be closed on the *fifteenth* (or *15th*) of June.

    Note: If ordinal numbers can be written as one or two words, they are written as words. Longer ordinal numbers and dates are expressed in figures.

    My client celebrated his fifty-second birthday.
    We will celebrate the 175th anniversary of statehood.

- Time. While time designations using *a.m.* or *p.m.* are preferred, it is also correct in some instances to use *o'clock.* The expression *o'clock* is generally used with words such as *tonight, in the afternoon*, and so on. When used, the time is always spelled out.

    seven thirty o'clock in the evening
    nine o'clock tomorrow morning

    Times of day followed by a.m. or p.m. are expressed in figures.

    12:45 a.m.   9:15 p.m.

    Note: Either *A.M.* and *P.M.* or *a.m.* and *p.m.* is correct; be certain the form is consistent throughout the document. No space is used between the *a* or *p* and the *m.*

Use proofreaders' marks to indicate the correct usage of numbers in the following paragraph.

> Angela Swarthmore, whom we hired on July 15th last
> year, travels coast to coast several times a month.
> She is still fascinated by the fact that she can leave
> New York's LaGuardia Airport at 9 o'clock and arrive
> in Los Angeles at 11:30 A. M., just in time for lunch.
> On her recent trip she celebrated her 35th birthday.
> On the twenty-third of August she will make her first
> trans-Atlantic flight. That date also marks the 3rd
> anniversary of her joining the company.

Check your work in the Answer Key.
Review Principle 4 if you had any difficulty.

MASTERY CHECKPOINT ONE

Use proofreaders' marks to indicate the correct usage of numbers in the following short paragraphs.

1. Our order clearly stated "17 plotter cartridges in assorted colors"; we received only seven, all red. Please ship the remaining 10 in assorted colors (other than red) via Express Mail to our home office at 1 Madison Avenue.

2. Two thousand forty-three respondents agree that our Tel-desk disks are the best on the market. This year we have already shipped 7,115 10-disk cartons (or 1/10 of all disks sold) to leading computer dealers.

Check your work in the Answer Key.

MASTERY CHECKPOINT TWO

Use proofreaders' marks to indicate the correct usage of numbers in the following short paragraphs.

1. Please check the correctness of our Invoice No. Four Hundred Five. The correct price on the binders is $4.75 not 7.45; the correct price on fillers is $1.23 not 1.32. The correct discount for prompt payment should be 3.5 percent not 3%.

2. If you print your brochure on twenty lb. bond paper, you will increase its usefulness. We can have the finished copies for you next Friday, April 15th. Call me after 9 o'clock that morning, and we will arrange delivery.

Check your work in the Answer Key.

Proofreading numbers and number-intensive copy requires special attention. Here are some other techniques for proofreading the accuracy of numbers and number formats:

- Proof the text to ascertain that numbers are consistent with other known facts.

    Your sales report is due on Monday, July 27. (Verify that July 27 is actually a Monday.)
    The customer purchased ten copier cartridges: three black, four blue, and four brown. (3 + 4 + 4 = 11)

- Check extensions, as well as totals, on documents such as bills of sale, purchase orders, etc.

12	calendars	@3.00	36.00
4	holders	@1.50	5.00
24	message pads	@ .30	7.20
1	Durapen	@7.50	7.50
	Total Order		55.70

(The total is a correct addition of the numbers entered, but notice that 4 x 1.50 is 6.00, not 5.00.)

- Use chronological order when listing items that are identified by number. This list lacks a logical sequence if all invoices are retrieved by number:

    Invoice No. 37589-0
    40812-0
    38313-0
    39225-0

- Align Roman numerals on the right.

Incorrect	**Correct**
I.	I.
II.	II.
III.	III.
IV.	IV.
V.	V.

- Lists of numbers are aligned at the decimal point.

Incorrect	Correct
4.50	4.50
14.34	14.34
753.90	753.90
0.67	0.67

Document 1: The following is number-intensive copy. Use proofreaders' marks to edit any numbers that are expressed in a form not consistent with the above guidelines.

```
     My sales report for June 15 does not balance.  Would
you please check the following items for me for a possible
error I may have overlooked.

P.O. No.  Date of Sale  Amount of Sale     Tax     Total Due
78901        6-1-86        1,578.35       63.24    1,614.59
79810        6-2-86          735.21       30.19      765.40
78920        7-3-86        2,539.00      102.87    2,641.78
78954        6-5-86          813.02       37.67      850.69
78855        6-7-86        3,810.05      119.66    3,929.71
```

Document 2: Scan the organization chart at the top of page 165. Use proofreaders' marks to indicate any errors. It was prepared from the following list:

Chairman	G.B. Johannsen
President	Margaret J. Johannsen (reports to chairman)
Vice president	Peter Kolinsky (reports to president)
Secretary	Sandra Levine (reports to president)
Treasurer	Arthur MacKenzie (reports to president)

Document 2

```
                    WEIMER ELECTRONICS INC
              Organization Chart -- April 10, 19XX

┌──────────────┐ ┌──────────────┐ ┌──────────────┐ ┌──────────────┐ ┌──────────────┐
│ MARGARET J.  │ │   PETER      │ │   SANDRA     │ │   ARTHUR     │ │   G.B.       │
│ JOHANNSON    │ │   KOLINSKY   │ │   LEVINE     │ │   MACKENZIE  │ │   JOHANNSEN  │
│ PRESIDENT    │ │   VICE       │ │   SECRETARY  │ │   TREASURER  │ │   CHAIRMAN   │
│              │ │   PRESIDENT  │ │              │ │              │ │              │
└──────────────┘ └──────────────┘ └──────────────┘ └──────────────┘ └──────────────┘
```

Document 3: Proofread the following memo for correct parallel structure as well as accuracy and consistency in the use of numbers. Use proofreaders' marks to indicate errors.

memorandum

to: Frank Kovacs   **date:**   July 10, 19XX

from: Suzette Armour   **subject:**   SECURITY CHANGES

The Security Task Force has recommended that the new security measures be implemented no later than August 15, 19XX. The following steps need to be taken to meet that deadline.

1. 125 sensor badges to be ordered at $7.00 each.

2. Three sensor readers need to be installed at the following locations:

   A. In the hall leading to Suite Ten
   B. At the shipping entrance
   C. At the subplaza entrance

3. All 350 employees need to be updated on the changes.

4. Our order of April 30, 19XX, from I-VU Products must be increased to seven uniforms and 16 communicators.

5. If possible, install 15 30-lb. viewers, preset to activate at eight a.m.

6. Determine what % of employees have clearance at present.

smt

Document 4: Proofread the following short article for any errors in format or language covered in Chapters 1 to 9. Use proofreaders' marks to indicate errors.

TELECOMMUTING: TODAYS HOME OFFICES

Telecommuters are either people who work at home or at an alternative work cite. The concept of telecommuting has been around for more than a decade, however, the interest has always been greater then the practice. What have we learned about telecommuting in those years?

Advantages

One of the primary advantages have been that the company can draw from a more experienced wider pool of job candidates.

In other words, there is a number of persons who are not willing to work from 9 to 5 at a specific location. These are people with highly-valued job skills who, for many reasons, choose to spend more time at home.

There is also some evidence that improved productivity results from working at home because employees choose their own best times to work which tend to be their most productive.

One of the measureable results are savings in office space. Office space in most large cities runs from $3,000 to $6,000. per professional worker.

The Other Side

According to many managers telecommuting also has its disadvantages. Many managers feel that they loose control when their workers are not in the office. Telecommuters report that they miss the camaraderie of the workplace. While the resulting disadvantages of the home office is still unknown it is a growing trend in todays workforce.

Document 5: The following draft of a form letter was keyed by a new employee in your office. Use proofreaders' marks to indicate errors.

We have instituted a new billing system for all accounts.

The soul purpose of this system is to make it as easy as

possible for our customers' to avoid unnecessary charges.

The following procedures are affective November first,

19XX.

    Accounts paid within fifteen days of shipping = five
    percent discount
    Accounts paid with 30 days of shipping = no billing
    charge
    Accounts paid within 31-45 days of shipping = 2%
    billing charges
    Accounts paid within 45-690 days of shipping = 3%
    billing charges
    Accounts paid after 61 days of shipping = 5% billing
    charge
    note: bILLING CHARGE TO BE ASSESSED ON TOTAL BILL

    These charges may seem some what high, however, we

believe the advantages of paying promptly outway the

advantages of delaying payment. We look fforeward to

serving you even more efficiently in the future.

    If you have questions about these changes, please call

me collect at (206) 555-28828.

PERFORMANCE GOALS

UPON COMPLETING THIS UNIT, YOU WILL BE ABLE TO:

- Enhance the format of documents according to generally accepted desktop publishing (DTP) design principles

- Edit short business documents for correct sentence structure, excessive wording, and correct details

- Apply common rules of effective business writing to business documents

UNIT
IV

EDITING BUSINESS DOCUMENTS

Your successful completion of the previous chapters enables you to move to a new level of proofreading: editing. Perhaps you are wondering what the difference is between proofreading and editing. Let's consult the dictionary for definitions.

As you recall, to *proofread* is "to read against the original manuscript for corrections." [1] To *edit* is "to prepare for publication or presentation, as by correcting or adapting." [2]

Even though these definitions denote two different levels of activities, the two terms are often used interchangeably. That is probably because the same person is often responsible for both activities.

Upon completion of this chapter, you should feel very comfortable assuming responsibility as a proofreader and as an editor of newsletters.

Here are your goals for this chapter:

● Enhance your format reviewing skill by learning basic design principles of desktop publishing.
● Edit business documents for sentence fragments, run-ons, and misplaced modifiers.

EDITING FOR FORMAT AND CONTENT
NEWSLETTERS

Your ability to scan document formats will also move to a new level in this chapter as you learn some basic desktop publishing design principles. These are illustrated by a sample newsletter.

---

[1] *The American Heritage Dictionary.* Boston: Houghton Mifflin Company, 1985, p. 992.

[2] Ibid., p. 438.

A company newsletter can serve many purposes: it may be an internal communication; it may be designed for external public relations; or it may be distributed both internally and externally. It may consist of a single page or several pages. It is an important communication device requiring a high level of readability.

✔ Select a multiple-column format for purposes of readability rather than a single-column format.

✔ Include "white space" between columns, boxes, or graphics to enhance readability.

✔ Use the width of the column to determine the size of the typeface: the narrower the column, the smaller the typeface.

✔ Select a serif typeface for columnar text.

✔ Increase the effectiveness of your headlines in any of three ways:
- Set them in a larger typeface than that of the accompanying text.
- Set them in a sans serif typeface.
- Keep them short!

✔ Determine your justification style with the following pointers in mind:
- A flush-left, ragged-right alignment gives a feeling of openness.
- Justified columns tend to "darken" a page and are considered to be more difficult to read.

✔ Add extra space between paragraphs to further enhance readability.

✔ Use type enhancements such as boldface, italics, underlining, and all caps sparingly.

The following article is ready to be "pasted in" to a newsletter column. Refer to the Formatting Checkpoints on the previous page. What changes would you suggest?

```
PROOFREADER
     ...or EDITOR?
```

Have you ever wondered just what your role is? Are you a *proofreader*? Are you an *editor*? Or, like growing numbers of support staff, are you both?

What's the difference? The *proofreader* compares final copy to the original and checks for accuracy of obvious items such as numbers, totals, and statistics. The *editor* goes one step further--the editor reads for sense. The editor is an analyst: What is the writer trying to say? Has the message been clearly stated?

Editing adds an exciting dimension to your job. You can truly function as a member of the team.

Which are you? A *proofreader* or an *editor*?

Suggested changes:

1. _____
2. _____
3. _____
4. _____
5. _____

Check your work in the Answer Key at the back of this book.

USING LANGUAGE EFFECTIVELY
SENTENCE STRUCTURE

Read the following short paragraphs and note the highlighted text. These highlights illustrate common errors in sentence structure. Do you understand each error? This section provides a brief review of sentence structure for you.

```
    For your consideration.  The proposed changes are likely
to be costly.  In excess of $100,000.  One consideration will
be of prime importance.  Gaining the support of a majority of
the staff.

    Even though this proposal is costly, we will proceed with
initial planning, we feel certain that this plan or an
adaptation of it will be accepted.
```

Each sentence you write becomes a part of a larger, cohesive whole—a paragraph, a section, a chapter, and finally a complete document. Each sentence you write must be a single, complete element. These two statements may appear to relay obvious information, yet sentence fragments and run-on sentences are common errors in business documents. This section includes examples of these errors and gives you an opportunity to edit sentences as you develop your skill at the next level of proofreading—editing documents.

PRINCIPLES AND PRACTICE
SENTENCE STRUCTURE

Correcting poor sentence structure is perhaps the most important editing skill you will develop. Even the worst writing can be made understandable by eliminating incomplete thoughts or by separating sentences that contain too many thoughts. Misplaced modifiers are also confusing for the reader. The following principles will help you to develop these important editing skills.

▼ PRINCIPLE 1: Fragments and Run-ons

Fragments or thoughts that pack too much information into one sentence confuse the reader. The following guidelines should aid in your editing of such problem writing.

*   Use grammatically complete sentences in your writing, except in the least formal situations. Incomplete sentences are called *sentence fragments*. Look at this example.

Sentence followed by sentence fragment:

She said I was to chair the meeting. Although I don't know why I was her choice.

Rewritten sentence:

She said I was to chair the meeting although I don't know why I was her choice.

Note: Sentence fragments are often dependent clauses that can be corrected by simply changing the punctuation.

Acceptable sentence fragments:

Outstanding!   How sad!

Note: Often short exclamations are punctuated as short sentences and are acceptable in all but the most formal writing.

- A second type of faulty sentence structure is a *run-on sentence*—two or more sentences punctuated as a single sentence.

Run-on sentence:

You will receive preliminary reports in February for both projects, neither report will be complete until July.

Rewritten sentences:

You will receive preliminary reports in February for both projects, but neither report will be complete until July.
or
You will receive preliminary reports in February for both projects; neither report will be complete until July.
or
You will receive preliminary reports in February for both projects. Neither report will be complete until July.

Use proofreaders' marks to edit the structure of the following sentences.

1. Jan and Kerry attended the seminar, they found it very helpful.
2. Her promotion was unexpected at this time. Since it was not part of her performance review.
3. Even though I am in total disagreement with you.
4. We will be happy to review your proposal. If you will provide us with a complete description of the final product.
5. The team concept was not successful, few of our employees understood it.

Check your work in the Answer Key.

▼ PRINCIPLE 2: Modifiers

- Place modifiers as close as possible to the words they modify.

Dangling modifier:

Managing the office last week, the problems piled up for him. (Were the *problems* managing the office?)

Correct modifier:

Managing the office last week, he saw the problems pile up.

Misplaced modifier:

The assistant took her boss to lunch, who was leaving next week. (Who was leaving—the *assistant* or the *boss*?)

Correctly placed modifier:

The assistant, who was leaving next week, took her boss to lunch.

- Make certain your modifiers serve as clear references.

Unclear modifier:

Roberta and Joyce could not agree on the final format. She felt strongly that an informal approach was best. (Who is *she*?)

Clear modifier:

Roberta and Joyce could not agree on the final format. Joyce felt strongly that an informal approach was best.

Use proofreaders' marks to edit the modifiers in the following sentences.

1. Stepping from the elevator, the door closed on her foot.
2. Enclosed are two receipts for merchandise you have not received previously.
3. George's and Kevin's budgets were denied because he refused to include a 3 percent cut in overhead.

4. She only gets two weeks' vacation.
5. As our newest employee, it is my privilege to welcome you aboard.

Check your work in the Answer Key.

Use proofreaders' marks to edit the following short paragraphs.

MASTERY CHECKPOINT

1. Today I learned that Sharon Vincenzo and Elayne Crippen were suspended for insubordinate behavior. Can you verify whether she plans to take legal action?

2. The network will be installed next Monday. Which explains why we are not inputting this data until late next week. Francine Georges will work with our technicians for the next two weeks, they will find her to be a very competent trainer.

Check your work in the Answer Key.
If you had any difficulty, review Principles 1 and 2.

PERFORMANCE CHALLENGE
EDITING NEWSLETTERS

As your experience grows, you may find that you are both a proofreader and an editor. When you are able to fill both roles, you are extremely valuable to the writers in your organization. Adding to these skills a basic understanding of design and formatting principles commonly used in desktop publishing will only increase your value.

Document 1: Scan the proposed layouts for a page of a newsletter. Which one is more attractive to you? Justify your choice on the lines provided.

HEADLINE FOR A GREY, STATIC PAGE

Here is text without much white space, and it is difficult to tell one part of the page from another. Here is text without much white space, and it is difficult to tell one part of the page from another.

Here is text without much white space, and it is difficult to tell one part of the page from another.

Here is text without much white space, and it is difficult to tell one part of the page from another. Here is text without much white space, and it is difficult to tell one part of the page from another. Here is text without much white space, and it is difficult to tell one part of the page from another. Here is text without much white space, and it is difficult to tell one part of the page from another.

Here is text without much white space, and it is difficult to tell one part of the page from another. Here is text without much white space, and it is difficult to tell one part of the page from another. Here is text

without much white space, and it is difficult to tell one part of the page from another.

Here is text without much white space, and it is difficult to tell one part of the page from another. Here is text without much white space, and it is difficult to tell one part of the page from another.

Here is text without much white space, and it is difficult to tell one part of the page from another.

Here is text without much white space, and it is difficult to tell one part of the page from another. Here is text without much white space, and it is difficult to tell one part of the page from another. Here is text without much white space, and it is difficult to tell one part of the page from another. Here is text without much white space, and it is difficult to tell one part of the page from another. Here is text without much white space, and it is difficult to tell one part of the page from another.

Here is text without much white space, and it is difficult to tell one part of the page from another.

HEADLINE FOR A MORE READABLE PAGE

Here is text without much white space, and it is difficult to tell one part of the page from another. Here is text without much white space, and it is difficult to tell one part of the page from another. Here is text without much white space, and it is difficult to tell one part of the page from another.

Subhead to add interest

Here is text without much white space, and it is difficult to tell one part of the page from another. Here is text without much white space, and it is difficult to tell one part of the page from another. Here is text without much white space, and it is difficult to tell one part of the page from another.

Subhead to group text

Here is text without much white space, and it is difficult to tell one part of the page from another. Here is text without much white space, and it is difficult to tell one part of the page from another. Here is text without much white space, and it is

difficult to tell one part of the page from another. Here is text without much white space, and it is difficult to tell one part of the page from another. Here is text without much white space, and it is difficult to tell one part of the page from another.

Another subhead

Here is text without much white space, and it is difficult to tell one part of the page from another. Here is text without much white space, and it is difficult to tell one part of the page from another. Here is text without much white space, and it is difficult to tell one part of the page from

---

Document 2: Use proofreaders' marks to edit the following newsletter article for sentence structure and misplaced modifiers.

LITERACY IN AMERICA

Are you aware that every day hundreds of thousands of Americans struggle with reading and understanding what they read? On the job, in school, in the workplace, in everyday tasks.

The good news is that there is help for these people through volunteer agencies, these wonderful volunteers have opened the "reading eyes" of many thousands of Americans. The inability to read and the thousands of people who suffer from it can be wiped out in our society.

Document 3: Proofread and edit the following article for any errors covered to this point.

VDTs ARE A PANE IN THE NECK!

The person who uses a computer for long hours some times complain of health problems including head aches, anusea, and aching backs, necks and shoulders. Are any of these uncomfortable discomforts due to the fact that the person is using a VDT?

Considerable amounts of research has been done to determine if any serious health problems results from prolonged VDT usage, and the idea has been largely disproven. However, more and more health specialists do agree that some of the discomforts related to VDT usage are preventable. Prevention begins with the hardware, the monitor should be at eye level or slightly below. The desk top should be 25 to 27 inches above the floor. The chair should adequately support the back.

With the hardware properly positioned in place, the user can also contribute to "comfortable computing". He will find the following helpful:

1. Taking frequent breaks from the monitor. Looking at a spot high on the wall or ceiling greatly reduce eye fatigue.

2. Turning the head as far right or left as possible and nodding several times.

3. Lifting the shoulders into a shrugging position, hold them there for a few seconds, and then relaxing them slowly.

Nearly 80 million Americans suffer from some kind of back pain. VDT users need not add to that number!

Editing is a progressive skill—as document originators observe your skill developing, they will ask you to add light editing to your proofreading duties. Editing is a skill that is used only with permission. When you become a trusted editor, your job value as a proofreader increases greatly. On a personal level, the ability to edit is an important skill for you to develop as you move along your career path. This chapter will help you make that progress.

Here are your goals for this chapter:

- Enhance your editing skill by developing your ability to assess effective letters.
- Edit business documents for excessive wording.

EDITING FOR FORMAT AND CONTENT

BUSINESS LETTERS

As you are well aware, learning to write successful business letters and memos is an entire college course. The purpose here is not to teach you everything there is to know about writing. Rather, the intent is to give you information that you can apply to business letters to increase the possibility of their being read and responded to as the writer hopes.

For many years business correspondence specialists have taught that effective letters conform to specific principles. While the number and names of these principles vary among authorities, a common reference is the "Five Cs": clarity, completeness, correctness, courtesy, and conciseness. When your letters adhere to these principles, you are writing effective letters.

Study the following letter. The Formatting Checkpoints further explain the Five Cs.

AN EFFECTIVE LETTER

MARQUIS DESIGN
ASSOCIATES
7125 HARRIET AVENUE · MINNESOTA, MN 55419
PHONE: 612 · 927-7125 FAX: 612 · 929-7125

August 1, 19xx

Ms. Denise Kaiser
P.O. Box 455
Milwaukee, WI 53201

Dear Ms. Kaiser:

Thank you for your order #323 of July 25, 19xx. It will be shipped via Airport Express on August 5, 19xx.

We are excited about the major contract you have been awarded. You have worked hard, and you are beginning to reap the rewards. Congratulations!

If you find that you need any additional supplies as you begin work, please call us at 1-800-555-7700. Whenever possible, we will be happy to provide overnight shipping.

Once again, good luck! We look forward to supplying your paint needs in the very near future.

Sincerely,

Yolanda Cassidy
Contract Specialist

hgh

✔ The letter begins on a *courteous* note. The wording throughout is warm and polite.
✔ The first paragraph demonstrates *completeness, correctness*, and *clarity*.
✔ While the letter tone is warm, it is also *concise,* or brief.

Read each of the following sentences. The writing principle being emphasized is listed first. Rewrite the sentence to strengthen the application of the principle.

Note: While suggested sentences appear in the Answer Key, there may be many right answers. You may add facts of your own choosing to demonstrate the writing principle.

1. *Completeness:*
   Your order will be shipped next week.

   _____

2. *Correctness:*
   We have the following dates open: Monday, January 15; Tuesday, January 16; and Wednesday, January 18.

   _____
   _____

3. *Conciseness:*
   It has come to my attention that your job performance over the past six months or half year has been considerably below that of previous months.

   _____
   _____
   _____

4. *Courtesy:*
   Your complaint letter has been turned over to Helen Jackson, an experienced and knowledgeable investigator in our Customer Service Division.

   _____
   _____
   _____

5. *Clarity:*
   How do you think the change will be accepted by the group since it represents such a different perspective?

   _____
   _____

USING LANGUAGE EFFECTIVELY

CONCISE WORDING

Read the following text of a short letter. Note the highlighted segments. These highlights illustrate common occurrences of excessive wording. Do you understand each error? This section provides a brief review of improved, concise wording for business documents.

> We are **in receipt of** your application for a position as junior controller. **Due to the fact that** we are under a hiring freeze, we **are not in a position** to interview you **at this point in time.** Your qualifications are impressive, and we are certain you will soon find **a position to your liking.**
>
> **Thanking you for** thinking of XYZ Corporation as you begin your career, we wish you the best.

The editing skill of using as few words as possible is one that must be applied carefully. First, additional words are sometimes used deliberately to soften the message. Second, writing in as few words as possible may lead to a curt tone rather than convey a concise message. The careful writer walks a fine line between the two.

At the same time, the use of unnecessary words may lead the reader to say, "Get to the point!" As an editor, you should recognize common occurrences of excessive wording. These include:
* Wordy and/or outdated expressions
* Redundant expressions

PRINCIPLES AND PRACTICE

CONCISE WORDING

Study each of the lists in Principles 1 and 2. These represent only samples of excessive wording. Other reference sources and business writing books contain longer lists.

Do you note any expressions that appear in your writing? Now that you have seen other examples, can you add to the list from your own writing? These are the occurrences you want to be especially aware of and work to eliminate.

▼ PRINCIPLE 1: Excessive Wording and Outdated Expressions

Some phrases become overused and meaningless while others become dated.

Excessive wording	Concise wording
at this point in time	now
can be in a position to	can
due to the fact that	because
each and every one	every one
for the purpose of	for
in a position to	can
in the near future	soon
inasmuch as	since
make inquiry regarding	ask about
meets with our approval	we approve
our experience indicated	we learned

Outdated expressions	Concise expressions
at your earliest convenience	soon
Dear Sirs	Gentlemen
Dear Sirs and Madams	Ladies and Gentlemen
enclosed please find	enclosed is
in receipt of	have
thanking you for	thank you
thank you in advance	thank you
under separate cover	separately

The following sentences contain some of the wordy expressions listed as well as others. Edit each sentence to make it more concise.

1. The meeting has been called for the purpose of reviewing the tentative labor agreement.
2. Thank you in advance for your cooperation.
3. Please send the confirmation back to me under separate cover.
4. Enclosed please find your corrected statement. Please pay the amount due at your earliest convenience.
5. Due to the fact that our expanded facilities will not be complete until August, we are not in a position to purchase office furniture at this point in time.

Check your work in the Answer Key.

▼ PRINCIPLE 2: Redundancies

Redundant expressions (two or more words that mean the same thing) creep into both our spoken and written language undetected. If we take time to listen to these expressions, we find that they are used to emphasize a point or to make certain the listener understands our meaning. In both instances, they are unnecessary.

The following list of common redundancies will help increase your awareness. Note that only the italicized word is needed.

advance *planning*	*reiterate* again
basic *fundamentals*	*repeat* again
completely *finished*	*revert (refer)* back
free *gratis*	*small (large)* in size
new *innovation*	the only other *alternative*
past *experience*	true *facts*

The following sentences contain some of the redundancies listed above as well as other examples. Edit each sentence to delete redundant expressions.

1. The only other alternative is to revert back to our original production method.
2. The consensus of opinion is that the true facts may never be known.
3. Our first priority is to use our past experiences in solving the problem.
4. The new warehouse should be completely finished by June 15.
5. The group meeting will give you an opportunity to reiterate again your feelings about the issue.

Check your work in the Answer Key.

The following short letter has several examples of excessive and outdated words and phrases. Edit the copy to delete these occurrences.

Dear Sirs:

We are in receipt of your letter regarding your past due account. We have referred back to all of the past year's transactions; at this point in time we are unable to locate the amount in question.

Past experience suggests that the amount was simply entered twice. One piece of information would be helpful to us--the invoice number of the transaction.

If you would send this back to me as soon as possible, I am certain the matter can be settled quickly. Let me repeat again, as I told you earlier, you are a valued customer. We will do all we can to resolve the issue.

Thank you in advance for your cooperation.

Sincerely yours,

Check your work in the Answer Key.

PERFORMANCE CHALLENGE
EDITING BUSINESS LETTERS

Proofreading typically involves comparison: Does the finished copy match the original copy? It often includes the further step of checking the accuracy of figures or statistics. It rarely involves reading copy for meaning. That is editing. Editing is analytical. It involves reading copy for meaning and for its adherence to the principles of good business writing. Editing is seldom easy!

Document 1: Edit the following text of a short letter for its adherence to good writing principles covered in this chapter.

We are in receipt of your detailed assessment of the county hearing in the environmental waste matter on June 15, 19xx. Frankly, we are totally confused.

Does this assessment represent the actual proceedings, or does it represent your opinion of the proceedings? What is the next step they will take?

You must clarify this matter for us before we are willing to respond as you requested.

Document 2: Edit the following body of a letter to eliminate excess wording, outdated phrases, and redundancies.

Thanks for making inquiry about the status of the child care provision under current negotiation. There is nothing new to report to you at this point in time.

We continue to pursue a course of providing an on-site child care facility for full-time employees within the next 12 months. Inasmuch as this proposal is a new innovation for us and will involve a considerable large amount of money, it is being studied very carefully.

We hope to have the proposal completely finished in the near future. Each and every one of you will hear from us as soon as possible thereafter.

Document 3: Proofread and edit the following document for any errors in format or language.

November 20, 19xx

Mr. Jake Armstrong
Convair Corporation
8877 Bellevue Highway
Seattle, WA 98119

Dear Jack:

   Its that time again! Our annual manager's seminar has been scheduled for the Bay Area during the week of January 12.

   Preliminary arrangements are for the first session to be held on Wednesday, January 13; but that date is not firm. Therefore, please keep your calender clear for the entire week until the dates can be finalized. Which I anticipate will be within the next ten days. If you have a scheduling problem, please call me immediately.

   Your early reports indicate that you have had a very good year, I congradulate you!

Sincerely,

Joni Beckett
Seminar Coordinator

eer

The principles of letter writing you applied in Chapter 11 will be helpful as you continue to develop your editing skill with memos. As with letters, editing memos is a skill that you will apply if the writer wishes or requests you to do so. Understanding the principles of memo writing is critical because many more memos are written than letters. When you complete this chapter, you will feel quite confident that you can assess the potential effectiveness of memos.

Here are your goals for this chapter:

- Further enhance your editing skill by developing your ability to assess effective memos.
- Read and edit business documents for details.

EDITING FOR FORMAT AND CONTENT

MEMOS

Memos are used to communicate internally. Therefore, they are more direct and more concise than letters. While their tone is never discourteous, the message does not include some of the "nice things" that might be said in a business letter. Memos might be described as "all business"!

Study the following memo. The Formatting Checkpoints highlight the important parts of the memo message.

AN EFFECTIVE MEMO

```
MEMORANDUM


To:        Corporate Office Staff

From:      Michael McKenna

Date:      February 15, 19xx

Subject:   STOCK OPTION PLAN

I am pleased to announce that effective March 1,
19xx, corporate office staff will be eligible to
purchase shares of commmon stock equal to 8.5
percent of their gross salary through payroll
deduction.  This is an increase of 1 percent.

If you wish to effect this or any other change in
your direct stock purchases, you can obtain the
necessary payroll form from Ellie Magoo at Ext.
771. Remember that payroll changes can be made
only during the following periods of each year:

  March 1 - March 15
  July 1 - July 15
  September 1 - September 15
  December 1 - December 15

If you have not previously taken advantage of the
stock option plan, talk to Ellie or one of your
colleagues.  You will find that the results have
been excellent.

vnp
```

FORMATTING CHECKPOINTS

✔ The most important information is in the first paragraph.
✔ The second paragraph supports the main message of the first paragraph.
✔ The last paragraph conveys one final bit of information.
✔ The paragraphs are short and very readable.
✔ The list format in the second paragraph aids readability.

Read each of the following pairs of memo paragraphs. Select the more effective one of each pair. Write the reason for your choice on the lines below.

Sample opening paragraph:
1. Your vacation request was received in our office yesterday. Since your request is somewhat unusual, we will have to refer it to the Employee Relations Committee at its next meeting.
2. Your request for three added vacation days has been sent to the Employee Relations Committee for consideration at its April 13 meeting.

Choice: _____
Reasons: _____
_____

Sample second (supporting) paragraph:
1. Your order will be shipped on Monday, September 23, via Speedy Xpress. The two items that are on back order (see attached copy) will be shipped no later than October 5.
2. We hope to give you our usual efficient service and plan to ship your order no later than Monday, September 23. As you know, the receipt of items on back order is always unpredictable; but we hope we can ship within two weeks after the above date.

Choice: _____
Reasons: _____
_____

Sample closing paragraph:
1. Jane Elliott, Travel Department supervisor, will be happy to help you if these arrangements are not satisfactory.
2. As you know, we like to please our clients. Just call our Travel Department if you need to change this itinerary.

Choice: _____
Reasons: _____
_____

Check your work in the Answer Key.

Read the following note. The highlighted text illustrates details missing from the note. Did you notice the missing details as you read the note?

A Note from the Desk of

Betti Ann Killarney

Ruth:

Let's get together to discuss the legal action Marjorie Rollinson has indicated she is going to file. I find the allegations very hard to believe, but we can't take them lightly.

Perhaps Norton Cummings should meet with us. **My office is available.**

What is the date of the meeting? The time?
Is the writer assuming that Ruth knows about the legal action?
Should Norton Cummings be included or not?
Is the office available at all times?

This section provides an opportunity for you to improve your skill in editing for details.

Careful proofreaders sometimes concentrate so intensely on reading for errors that they forget to proof for missing details or correctness. These errors and omissions are costly because the reader and writer must spend extra time clearing up the details. The experienced proofreader or editor always makes one final check to be certain that all details are included and correct.

Never assume missing details. When appropriate, check the accuracy of the details. If you, as the proofreader, find information missing, you can be quite sure the reader will also.

PRINCIPLES AND PRACTICE
DETAILS

Assume that your responsibilities include planning meetings. One of the easiest ways to accomplish this is to develop a worksheet that can be used to verify the details of all meetings.

SAMPLE MEETING WORKSHEET

```
                  MEETING WORKSHEET

_____  Time              _____  Response
_____  Date              _____  Writing supplies
_____  Place             _____  Refreshments
_____  Participant names _____  AV equipment
_____  Leader            _____  Room arrangement
_____  Contact person    _____  Materials for
                                   distribution
_____  Agenda            _____  Participant preparation

Other details_____

_____

_____

_____

_____
```

The sample worksheet lists the items that often need to be considered when planning a meeting. You will use the worksheet by checking the items that apply to the meeting you are planning. It can serve as a point of reference throughout the planning process.

Edit each of the following three memos announcing a meeting of department supervisors. Refer to your checklist, and write which important details are missing.

1. The monthly meeting of department supervisors will be held on Monday at 2 p.m. in the Susquehanna Room at the Berkshire Motor Inn.

   The major item on the agenda is staffing. Please prepare ten copies of two-year staffing projections for your department.

   _____

   _____

2. The monthly meeting of department supervisors is scheduled for Wednesday, September 15, at 1 p.m. As usual, in order to avoid interruptions, we will meet at the Berkshire Motor Inn.

   The major item on the agenda is a review of last year's sales. As you know, we fell short of our projections; therefore, I want to spend our time analyzing "soft" areas and developing plans for strengthening these.

   If for any reason you cannot attend this meeting, please call my secretary at Ext. 2450 before September 16.

   _____

   _____

3. The monthly meeting of department supervisors is scheduled for Thursday, September 17, 1-3 p.m.

   Since I plan to present the final budget for next year, each of you is asked to give this meeting priority scheduling.

   _____

   _____

Check your work in the Answer Key.

PERFORMANCE CHALLENGE
EDITING MEMOS

The growth of your proofreading skills should be evident as you add editing skills to the production of effective business documents. Multiple readings are often required as you proofread and edit for content, grammar, and format. The combination of critical thinking and a trained eye for checking details makes your work extremely important in any organization.

Proofread and edit the following memo for missing or inaccurate details. Use proofreaders' marks to indicate errors.

MEMORANDUM

TO: Marvin Gottlieb
          Jennifer Doran

FROM: Clarence McDevitt

DATE: July 7, 19xx

SUBJECT: MONTHLY REPORT FORMAT

As of today, I have received monthly reports from 11
of our 16 departments. I have found that each of these
requires three to four hours to review due to
inconsistency of format.

To be specific:

* Departments 1, 3, 5, and 7 used our new report
  software.
* Departments 2, 4, 6, 8, 9, and 10 did not use the
  new software and prepared the reports according to
  individual preferences.

I like to give personnel every opportunity to adjust
to changes on their own. However, I must insist that
the new software be installed and used, effective
immediately.

To facilitate this, I am scheduling a second users'
workshop for two weeks from today, July 28. Each
department must sent the appropriate person(s) to
this workshop.

bxm

Document 1: Edit the text of the following short memo for its adherence to good memo writing principles.

```
MEMORANDUM


TO:        Ann Marie Fernandez

FROM:      Linda Pottington

DATE:      Decmeber 15, 19xx

SUBJECT:   CONTRACT PROVITION SEC. III, ¶5

You certainly raised an interesting question when you
questioned the relevance of the above-cited contract
item. I spent the better part of a day trying to
track its origins.

Joe Klovac, Shipping Department, finally told me that
he thought it had been added shortly after the Korean
War when a number of veterans were returning and
their status was uncertain. That's as good an
explanation as I could find!

In any event, it is no longer applicable and will be
eliminated, upon approval of the Employees Committee.

olo
```

Document 2: Use proofreaders' marks to indicate any needed changes in the following memo.

MEMORANDUM

TO: John M. Nelson, VP

FROM: Lee Iverson, VP & Gen. Manager

SUBJECT: New Accountt Manager Position

DATE: May 15, 19xx

In the ABQ Position Report, I outlined the rational behind the request for an additional account manager by September or October in the fall. The purpose of this memo is to provide more details regarding that request.

<u>Title Experience Level</u>
While a banker from this area with 4 to 5 years of lending experience would be preferable, neither my interviewing nor that of Berkeley Associates has turned up a suitable candidate from this area. We will continue to keep our eyes open for a good local man, however.

<u>Function</u>
The primary main function of the additional account manager would be to develope incremental loan business by calling on assigned prospects and referrral sources. We need a confidant, outgoing person who is flexible yet persistent enought to learn how to do business the Upper Midwest region of the country.

    When the new person develops a potential local transaction piece of business, he can work closely with both Jean and me in putting the transaction together, getting it approved, and follow up. An emphases on training and production would exist during the first 12 to 18 months here.

If any farther details are needed, please let me know.

hhg

Document 3: Proofread and edit the following document. Use proofreaders' marks to indicate errors.

---

memorandum

to: Database Users   **from:**   Leeza Roberts

date: November 11, 19xx   **subject:** VERSION 3.0

In response to requests from many of you, a new updated version of our database will be available beginnning December 1.

To help acquaint you with the new features, two-hour seminars have been schedule as follow.

    Tuesday, November 20, 9:00 a.m.
    Thursday, November 22, 10:00 a.m.
    Tuesday, November 26, 1:00 p.m.
    Tuesday, November 26, 2:30 p.m.

An additional session will be scheduled on December 1st if at least five persons request it.

Please bring with you the following computer items: a blank formatted disk, pages twenty through thirty of your current training manual, and a sample entry from your current database.

ert

Y ou are now ready to use all of the skills you have developed as you have worked through the text. This assignment will give you an opportunity to do that.

Assume that you are employed as a proofreader by Seminar Specialists Inc. You have total responsibility for all printed documents. Quite an assignment, don't you agree? But you are ready!

The assignment consists of ten interrelated exercises. In other words, all names and titles are to be consistent throughout the assignment. Any one document may depend on a previous one for its content. You are truly expected to "bring it all together."

To assist you in completing the assignment successfully, you will want to read the short notes at the beginning of each exercise. Your textbook will serve as your reference.

Exercise 1: This is your guide to all employees and titles. The first copy is a corrected copy; the second copy is presumably a final document. Do you agree? As with all exercises, use proofreaders' marks to indicate errors and inconsistencies.

Performance Mastery Exercise 1—corrected copy

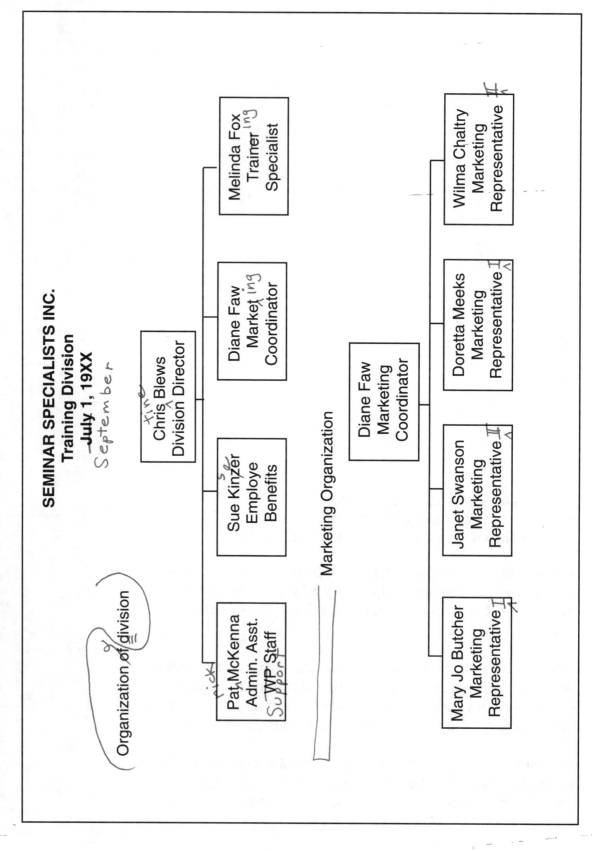

SEMINAR SPECIALISTS INC.
Training Division
~~July 1, 19XX~~
September

Organization of ~~division~~ _(circled)_

Chris Blews
Division Director
(time)

Pat McKenna
Admin. Asst.
~~WP Staff~~ *Support*

Sue Kinzer
Employe*s*
Benefits

Diane Faw
Market*ing*
Coordinator

Melinda Fox
Trainer *ing*
Specialist

Marketing Organization

Diane Faw
Marketing
Coordinator

Mary Jo Butcher
Marketing
Representative I

Janet Swanson
Marketing
Representative II

Doretta Meeks
Marketing
Representative I

Wilma Chaltry
Marketing
Representative II

Performance Mastery Exercise 1—final copy

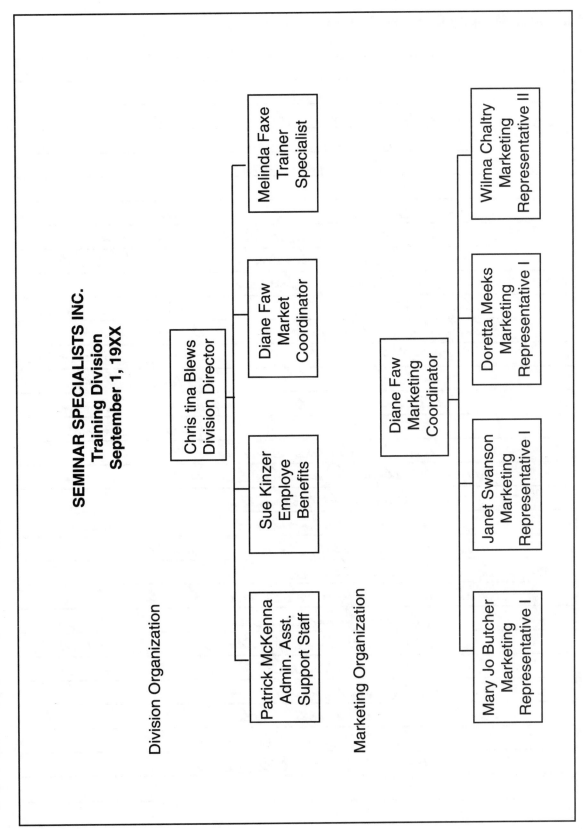

SEMINAR SPECIALISTS INC.
Training Division
September 1, 19XX

Division Organization

Chris tina Blews
Division Director

Patrick McKenna
Admin. Asst.
Support Staff

Sue Kinzer
Employe
Benefits

Diane Faw
Market
Coordinator

Melinda Faxe
Trainer
Specialist

Marketing Organization

Diane Faw
Marketing
Coordinator

Mary Jo Butcher
Marketing
Representative I

Janet Swanson
Marketing
Representative I

Doretta Meeks
Marketing
Representative I

Wilma Chaltry
Marketing
Representative II

Exercise 2: The keyed copy was prepared from the handwritten copy. Is it ready for distribution?

Performance Mastery Exercise 2—handwritten copy

Agenda
Seminar Specialists, Inc., Annual Meeting
Sectional Meeting: Training Division
September 20, 19 xx

9:00-9:15	Introductions	Sue Kinzer
9:15-10:00	Salaried Personnel Status	Robert Young
	Hourly Personnel Status	Terri Garth
10:00-11:00	Team Planning Sessions	
	Support Staff	Patricia McKenna
	Employee Benefits	Sue Kinzer
	Marketing	Diane Faw
	Training	Melinda Hay
11-12:15	Facilities Update	Nancy Chevron
		Ken McKenzie
12:00-1:30	Lunch: Conference Room	

"How to Develope Team Leaders and Team Members"
Sara O'Brien, Toastmasters International

1:30-3:00	Section Workshops (one half hour each)

Room A: Successful Seminars Begins With Planning
Room B: Cross-Cultural Awareness
Room C: Location, Location, Location!

3:00-3:30	Employee-Benefits Update	Sue Kinzer
	Presentation of Annuity Package	John Yee
		Metroplex Financial Planners
3:45-5:00	Closing Session	

"Seminar Specialists—Lets Go into the Future!"
Christine Bleuvs
Department Director

Performance Mastery Exercise 2—keyed copy

```
                            AGENDA

          SEMINAR SPECIALISTS, INC., ANNUAL MEETING

          Sectional Meeting:  Training Division

                   September 20, 19XX


9:00-9:15          Introductions                    Sue Kinzer

9:15-10:00         Salaried Personnel Status      Robert Young
                   Hourly Personnnel Status         Terri Garth

10:00-11:00        Team Planning Sessions
                   Support Staff               Patrick McKenna
                   Employee Benefits               Sue Kinzer
                   Marketing                        Diane Faw
                   Training                        Melinda Fax

11-12:15           Facilitys Update             Nancy Chevron
                                                  Ken McKenzie

12:00-1:30         Lunch:  Conference Room
            "How to Develope Team Leaders and Team Members"
              Sara O'Brien, Toastmasters International

1:30-3:00          Section Workshops (one half hour each)
                   Room A:  Successful Seminars Begins With Planning
Room B:  Cross-Cultural Awareness
                   Room C:  Location, Location, Location!

3:00-3:30          Employee-Benefits Update         Sue Kinzer
                   Presentation of Annuity Package    John Yee
                                      Metroplex Finaincial Planners

3:45-5:00          Closing Sessions
             "Seminar Specialists—Lets Go into the Future!"
                        Christine Blews
                        Department Director
```

Exercise 3: The January 1, 1993, roster was correct at the time of its printing. Of course, changes do occur within a year's time; these are detailed on the second document. One of your word processors prepared the January 1, 1994, copy. Is it correct?

Performance Mastery Exercise 3

EMPLOYEE ROSTER
January 1, 1993

SOFTWARE SPECIALISTS INC. — TRAINING DIVISION
Home Office (Full- and Part-Time)

CURRENT EMPLOYEE	SS #	ADDRESS	HIRE DATE	DEPT	INITIAL SALARY	INITIAL DEPT	CURRENT SALARY
ACHINSON J T	379-03-5156	5156 MARCH, ATLANTA 30042	10-15-87	MARKETING	21,200	MARKETING	27,900
BARLOW C B	375-01-8917	4501 FIRST, ATLANTA 30311	7-15-88	WP	19,500	WP	23,350
BARKER JOHN	288-32-1259	6565 CUSTER, BELVEDERE 30032	8-15-90	ADMIN	35,300	ADMIN	41,500
COX NANCI	386-90-3517	205 ASH, SMYRNA 30080	7-27-92	WP	19,500	ADMIN	25,300
CZECHI MARCI	285-30-8712	7801 LANIER, DEKALB 30033	8-1-91	TRAINING	28,200	TRAINING	31,300
DARBY JOSEPH	223-07-1547	PO BOX 334, ATLANTA 30305	1-1-90	TRAINING	29,500	TRAINING	35,100
EXETER PEGGY	335-87-8989	787 FIRST #225, EASTPOINT 30309	6-15-87	TRAINING	31,200	TRAINING	36,700
FOX WILLIAM	335-90-3857	12125 MASON, DECATUR 30335	3-10-91	ADMIN	39,500	ADMIN	46,200
HARRISON SYDNEY	221-08-5152	31290 ROBINWOOD, ATLANTA 30143	6-15-90	COMM	33,400	COMM	37,350
JACOBI LEVI	015-85-8734	1515 EUCLID, ATLANTA 30010	9-1-93	CUSTODIAL	18,900	CUSTODIAL	19,900
MCHALE ANNIE	113-78-0093	90-A UNIVERSITY, COLLEGE PARK 30337	2-15-92	WP	19,300	WP	21,500
NANKOVITZ IVAN	335-90-2345	3757 MEREDITH, ATLANTA 30094	9-1-90	COMM	24,300	COMM	26,900
PRAVH SUDAH	224-37-6472	234 COLLEGE AVE, COLLEGE PARK 30337	12-15-91	TRAINING	29,000	TRAINING	31,400
RAVITZ CARRIE	242-37-7390	150 NORWALK #115, CENTREVILLE 30058	3-15-92	WP	19,700	WP	22,000
RODGERS KENNY	387-28-8349	NORVILLE PARK #25, DEKALB 30033	10-1-89	ADMIN	37,000	ADMIN	42,500
RUSCHE CARLA	145-97-0897	18576 JACKSON, BELVEDERE 30032	7-15-88	MARKETING	22,000	MARKETING	25,500
SARGENT NORMA	224-39-9025	3095 PARK, FUNSTON 30001	10-15-87	ADMIN	30,500	ADMIN	43,900
SIEBOLD LLOYD	375-67-8741	9524 PARK RIDGE, ATLANTA 30331	6-1-89	MARKETING	25,600	MARKETING	29,500
THOMASON LYDIA	190-80-7649	75 BENT TREE, ATLANTA 30024	7-15-90	WP	20,100	WP	23,100

```
CHANGES IN EMPLOYEE ROSTER JANUARY 1, 1994

Corrections:  Fox, William    Correct SS# is 353-90-3857
              Sargent, Norma   Correct street address is 3905
Changes:      Exeter, Peggy    Married name is Boni, Peggy
              Rusche, Carla    New surname is LeFite
              Thomason, Lydia  New department is Comm

Delete:  Ravitz, Carrie
```

```
Salary Changes:
ACHINSON  29,100          COX     25,000        HARRISON  39,500        PRAVH     33,400
BARLOW    24,750          CZECHI  32,750        JACOBI    20,500        RODGERS   44,150
BARKER    43,250          DARBY   37,250        LEFITE    27,100        SARGENT   46,200
BONI      38,500          FOX     49,100        MCHALE    23,000        SIEBOLD   32,100
                                                NANKOVITZ 28,300        THOMASON  25,200

Add:
Ramona Juarez            SS# 255-90-7654
567 Molena
Atlanta 30144            Hire date: 12/1/93       WP  20,000  (NO INCREASE)
```

SOFTWARE SPECIALISTS INC. — TRAINING DIVISION
Home Office (Full- and Part-Time)

EMPLOYEE	SS #	ADDRESS	HIRE DATE	INITIAL DEPT	INITIAL SALARY	CURRENT DEPT	CURRENT SALARY
ATCHINSON J T	379-03-5156	5156 MARCH ATLANTA 30042	10-15-87	MARKETING	21,200	MARKETING	29,100
BARLOW C B	375-01-8917	4501 FIRST ATLANTA 30311	7-15-88	WP	19,500	WP	24,750
BARKER JOHN	288-32-1259	6565 CUSTER BELVEDERE 300032	8-15-90	ADMIN	35,300	ADMIN	43,250
COX NANCI	386-90-3517	205 ASH SMYRNA 30080	7-27-92	WP	19,500	ADMIN	25,000
CZECH MARCI	285-30-8712	7801 LANIER DEKALB 30033	8-1-91	TRAINING	28,200	TRAINING	37,250
DARBY JOSEPH	223-07-1547	PO BOX 334 ATLANTA 30305	1-1-80	TRAINING	29,500	TRAINING	32,750
BONI PEGGY	335-87-8989	787 FIRST #225 EASTPOINT 30309	6-15-87	TRAINING	31,200	TRAINING	38,500
FOX WILLIAM	353-90-3855	12125 MASON DECATUR 30335	3-10-91	ADMIN	39,500	ADMIN	49,100.00
HARRISON SYDNEY	221-08-5152	31290 ROBINWOOD ATLANTA 30143	6-15-90	COMM	33,400	COMM	35,900
JACOBI LEVI	015-85-8734	1515 EUCLID ATLANTA 30010	9-1-93	CUSTODIAL	18,900	CUSTODIAL	20,500
JAUREZ RAMONA	255-90-7654	567 MOLENA ATLANTA 30144	12/1/93	WP	20,000		
MCHALE ANNIE	113-78-0093	90-A UNIVERSITY COLLEGE PARK 30337	2-15-92	VP	19,300	WP	23,000
NANKOVITZ IVAN	335-90-2345	3757 MEREDITH ATLANTA 30094	9-1-90	COMM	24,300	COMM	28,300
PRAVH SUDAH	224-37-6472	234 COLLEGE AVE COLLEGE PARK 30337	12-15-91	TRAINING	29,000	TRAINER	33,400
RODGERS KENNY	242-37-7390	NORVILLE PARK #25 DEKALB 30033	3-15-92	ADMIN	37,000	ADMIN	44,150
LEFITE CARLA	145-97-0897	18576 JACKSON BELVEDERE 30032	7-15-88	MARKETING	22,000	MARKETING	27,100
SARGENT NORMA	224-39-9025	3095 PARK FUNSTON 33905	10-15-87	ADMIN	30,500	ADMIN	46,200
SIEBOLD LLOYD	375-67-8741	9524 PARK RIDGE ATLANTA 30331	6-1-89	MARKETING	29,500	MARKETING	32,100
THOMASON LYDIA	190-80-7649	75 BENT TREE ATLANTA 30024	7-15-90	WP	20,100	COMM.	25,200

Exercise 4: Diane Faw asks you to proofread this FAX before it is sent. Remember—you are proofreading and doing light editing on all documents.

Performance Mastery Exercise 4

FAX TRANSMITTAL FORM

TO:	**Raymond Cassidy**	DATE:	**Mon., Sept. 2, 19XX**
FROM:	**Diane Faw**	TIME:	**9:30 a.m.**

The Accounting Office held a seminar in the Mountain Shadows conference room on Friday, August 31, beginning at 8:30 a.m. All arrangments for this meeting were made three months' in advance. The following items were requested:

        4 8-foot tables in a "U" arrangment
        No ashtrays
        An overhead projector and screen
        Coffee, juice and rolls at 10 a.m.

I checked the room at 8 a.m. and found the following:

        Six tables arranged in rows
        Dirty ashtrays
        An overhead projecter with no screen

I immediately called your office, and contacted a Doris Kingston, who offfered no assistance. She indicated she had no paper work for such a meeting. So I took care of the details so the meeting could begin.

Raymond, this meeting included one of our board members and two outside auditors. It was potentially very embarassing! Even if we had had no visitors, were all a part of the same team. We must work together at every opportunity. Would you please look into this matter and call me as soon as possible with an explaination and a plan to keep this reoccurring.

Exercise 5: One of your marketing specialists needs a copy of "Works Cited" for a presentation she is doing. What do you think of this copy?

Performance Mastery Exercise 5

WORKS CITED

Watson, Jane. *The Minute Taker's Handbook.* North Vancouver, B.C.;
      Self-Counsel Press, 1992.

Cann, Marjorie. *Canns' Keys to Better Parliamentary Procedure*
      Simplified. Mobile, AL: HB Publications, 1990.

McMahon, Tom. *Big Results: Strategic Event Planning for*
      Productivity and Profit. NTC Business Books, Lincolnwood,
      IL: 1990.

Frank, Milo. *How to run a successful meeting—in half the time.*
New York: Simon & Schuster, 1989.

Thomsett, Michael C. *The Little Black Book of Business Meetings.*
      New York: 1987, AMACOM, American Management Association

Devney, Darcy Campion. *Organizing Special Events and*
      Conferences: A Practical Guide for Business Volunteers and
      Staff. Sarasota, Florida: Pineapple Press, 1990.

Bethel, Sheila Murray. *How To Organize and Manage a Seminar:*
      What To Do and When To Do It. New York: Prentice-Hall,
      1987.

Munson, Lawrence S. *How to Conduct Training Seminars.* 1989.
      New York: McGraw-Hill, 1989.

Sturgis, Alice. *The Standard Code of Parlimentary Procedure, 3d*
Edition. New York: McGraw Hill, 1988.

Exercise 6: The news release was keyed from the rough draft copy. News releases must be accurate. Would you send this one out?

Performance Mastery Exercise 6—rough draft copy

Seminar Specialists Inc., an Atlanta based firm since 1987, ~~has recently announced~~ announces the building of a new office complex ~~in the rapidly growing~~ area adjacent to it's present location at 4500 Peachtree North. The 150,000 sq.ft. complex will consist of three major buildings. SSI ~~plans to occupy the largest headquarters~~ will building move its rapidly growing headquarters staff into the largest of the three. A "smart" conference center will be the core of the main floor of this building. This will enable SSI to accomodate clients who must currently rent space at various locations. The second building will have tenant and client services: restaurant, meeting rooms, mail facilities, and limited warehousing. Office suites ranging from 500 to 5,000 sq. ft. will be available for related industries in the third building . SSI was recently awarded the "Outstanding Minority-Owned Enterprise of the Year" award at the Annual Convention of Women Business Owners in the United States. Since its founding in 1987, it has experienced phenominal success and growth. Ground breaking ceremonies at the site is being planned for October 15. Occupany is scheduled for eighteen months from begining of construction.

Performance Mastery Exercise 6—news release

N E W S   R E L E A S E   RELEASE: Immediately

                                     CONTACT: Joannie Bliss
                                                    555-9090 X135

SSI ANNOUNCES EXPANSION

Atlanta, September 5, 19XX. Seminar Specialists, Inc., an Atlanta-based

firm since 1987, announces the building of a new office complex area adjacent to

its present location at 4500 Peach Tree North. The 150,000-sq.ft. complex will

consist of three major buildings. SSI move its' rapidly growing headquarters staff

into the largest of the three. A "smart" conference center will be the core of the

main floor of this building. This will enable SSI to accomodate clients who must

currently find space to rent at varying locations. The second building will have

tenant and client services: restaurant, meeting rooms, mail facilities and limited

warehousing. Office suites ranging from 500 to 5,000 sq. ft. will be available for

lease in the 3rd building.

SSI was recently awarded the "Outstanding Minority-Owned Enterprise of

the Year Award" at the annual convention of Women Business Owners in the

United States. Since its founding in 1987, it has experienced phenomenal

success and growth. Ground-breaking ceremonies at the building sight is being

planned for October 15. Occupany is scheduled for 18 months from the beginning

of construction.

Exercise 7: The letter was keyed from the instructions provided. Is it accurate in every detail?

Performance Mastery Exercise 7—instructions

From the desk of

SUE KINSER

Write a letter to Francis Konac of Fulton Life in response to his letter of August 15, 19XX. Attach the list of persons employed prior to January 1, 1990.

Confirm our understanding that these persons are eligible for additional optional coverage. The additional coverage will be paid for by the employee. Fulton Life will contact each of the eligible persons within the next 30 days and explain the coverage to them.

Fulton Life will notify our Payroll Department by January 15, 199X, of those who elect the coverage. Employee contributions will begin on February 1, 199X.

Performance Mastery Exercise 7—list

SEMINAR SPECIALISTS INC.
Employee Eligible for Optional Life Insurance
(Hire Dates Prior to 1/1/90)

Employee	Hire Date
Achinson, J. T.	1-15-87
Barlow, C. B.	7-15-88
Boni, Peggy	6-15-87
Darby, Joseph	1-1-90
Lefite, Carla	1-15-88
Rogers, Kenny	10-1-89
Seibold, Lloyd	6-1-89

Seminar Specialists Inc.

4500 Peachtree North ✦ Atlanta, Georgia 30010
404-555-9000 Fax 404-444-9900

September 20, 19XX

Francis Konac
Fulton Life Insurance Company
P.O. Box 565
Macon, GA 31201

Dear Frances

Enclosed is a list of SSI employees who were hired prior to January 1,
1990.

My understanding of this matter is:

1. Each of these persons are eligible to puchase
   additional optional life insurance.

2. Any additional premiums will be paid by the employer

3. Fulton Life will contact each of these persons in
   approximately 30 days to explain the optional
   coverage

5. Fulton Life will notify our Payroll Department of
   such election by January 15, 19XX; employee
   contributions will begin on February 1, 19XX.

Thank you in advance for your assistance in implementing this benifit
for our employees.

Sincerely,

Sue Kinzer
Employee Benefits

hgr

Attachment

Electronic Mail seminar@atl.zzz

Exercise 8: Some people realize their writing faults. This writer has asked you to proofread a draft copy. Do your thing!

Performance Mastery Exercise 8

DRAFT COPY

TITLE: SSI—WHATS ITS SECRET?   SSI, formally known as Seminar Specialists Inc. is truly really an "infant" in the seminar planning industry. In just 6 short years it has grown from a single-owner operation to a business enterprise. Doing more then $6,000,000 in business yearly at this point in time—and still growing! ¶ What is it's secret? Nationally known training specialist Elaine Newquist, the founder of Seminar Specialists sum it up concisely and succinctly: "CARE! We CARE about our clients, and we relieve them of all CARE when they have training or seminar needs!" ¶ Ms. Neuquist explains their process this way: "From the clients first contact, he is assigned to an individual training specialist. That specialist assumes all responsibility for determining and meeting the individual, unique needs of the client. That relationship ends only when the client no longer has a training or seminar need. In todays business environment, thats probably never"! ¶ SSI is a full service organization for training and seminar needs. The SSI staff arranges everything from coffee to evaluations. With the opening of their new "smart" conference center late next year, their ability to meet your training needs can only be enhanced. The consensus of opinion among clients of SSI is almost unanimous, "There services are worth every dollar we spent!"

Exercise 9: The questionnaire was prepared by one of your training specialists. Will you release it for printing?

Performance Mastery Exercise 9

SEMINAR SPECIALISTS INC.

QUESTIONAIRE FOR POTENTIAL CLIENTS

PURPOSE: To enable us to know you better as we work cooperatively with you to determine your training and/or seminar needs. Please answer each question thoughtfully; they are each designed to address one individual, particular area of training.

QUESTIONS:

1. Do you recognise an immediate training need with in your organization?

    ❑   Yes   ❑   No

    If "Yes," describe it briefly below on the lines.

    _____
    _____
    _____

2. Are you aware of an immediate seminar need for your employes?

    ❑   Yes   ❑   No

    If "Yes", describe it briefly.

    _____
    _____
    _____

3. Would you be interested in attending a session "Asssessing Training Needs in Todays Business Environment"?

    ❑   Yes   ❑   No

4. Would you be interested in meeting with your own individual training specialist from SIS?

    ❑   Yes   ❑   No

    If "yes," what is the best time of day to contact you? _____

5. Have you ever in the past previously contracted the services of a training/seminar specialist?

    ❑   Yes   ❑   No

Exercise 10: The meeting summary follows the agenda you proofread as Exercise 2. Is it consistent?

Performance Mastery Exerise 10

**SUMMARY OF THE SECTION MEETING: TRAINING DEPARTMENT
SEMINAR SPECIALISTS INC.**

September 20, 19XX

The annual sectional meeting of the Training Division of Seminar Specialists, Inc., was held in the ballroom of the Regency Suites Hotel on September 20th, 19XX. All employees were present.

The following special honored guests were introduced: Marcus Antonio, Special Assistent to the Governor, Lurinda Kennedy, Marketing Specialists from Seminars Inc., and Wallace O'Keefe, President of the Atlanta City Counsel.

Nancy Chevron and Ken McKensie presented an exciting update of the new facilities of SSI. Interim plans for occupancy of the present building was also reviewed.

Sue Kinzer reviewed the current employee benefits package as it is now in place. She then introduced John Yee from Metroplex Financial Planning who explained in detail the annuity package which will be available on January 1.

A continuing, ongoing growth in both salaried and hourly employees were reported by Robert Young and Terry Garth. It is possibly anticipated that SSI will increase their staff by 5% during the coming year of 199X.

Sara O'Brien, Toastmaster International, challenged the group with her presentation "Developing Team Leaders and Team Members".

Summarys of team planning sessions will be distributed to each team member within sixty days.

Recorders for sectional workshops are as follows:

Room A: Evelyn Orlando—Ext. 710
Room B: Andrew McFarland—Ext. 715
Room C: Marie Yong—X 717

The recorders for each workshop is to be contacted for summaries of the workshop.

Christina Blews, Division Director, reviewed the activities of the Training Division over the past year. The level of activity for the total staff have grown 15%. She challenged the group to share their dreams for the new "smart" conference center. Several of these will be studied farther.

Introduction, p. xiv

NOTICE TO ALL Sales PERSONNEL

Begining next monday, January 15, your monthly sales reports will be due on the 15th of each month. When the 15th falls on a week end, reports are due on the following Monday.

The new report forms, designed by your task force, are are now available from Sandi in Corporate Accounting.

Letter 1, p. 8 No. Too high on page

Letter 2, p. 9 No. Inconsistent spacing: Add a triple space before and after subject line; add two vertical spaces before signature line

Letter 3, p. 10 No. Paragraphs should not be indented

Letter 4, p. 11 No. Margins too wide: Use default (1") margins

Spelling practice, p. 15

1. arranging	2. actively	3. appropriately
4. receivables	5. deceive	6. lien
7. decreeing	8. deleting	9. accruing
10. management		

Spelling practice, p. 16

1. directories	2. customarily	3. employs
4. reliance	5. surveying	6. libraries
7. opportunities	8. policies	9. displaying
10. loyalties		

Spelling practice, p. 17

1. occurring	2. controlling	3. credited
4. efficiency	5. beginning	

Spelling practice, p. 18

1. exchangeable 2. utilize 3. exceed 4. complimentary 5. apologize
6. respectable 7. precede 8. recognize 9. transferable 10. dietary

Mastery Checkpoint One, p. 19

1. submitting, improving, actively
2. judgment, believing, inaccuracies, proficient

Mastery Checkpoint Two, p. 19

1. reasonable, eligible, emphasize, supplementary
2. receivable, itemize, payable, proceed

Formatting practice, p. 29

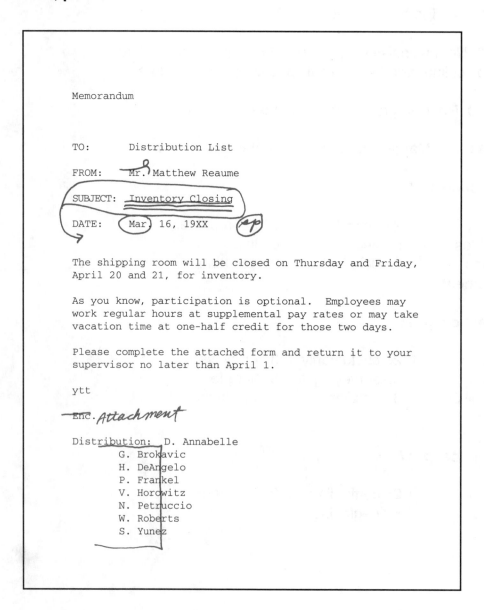

Memorandum

TO: Distribution List

FROM: Mr. Matthew Reaume

SUBJECT: Inventory Closing

DATE: Mar 16, 19XX

The shipping room will be closed on Thursday and Friday,
April 20 and 21, for inventory.

As you know, participation is optional. Employees may
work regular hours at supplemental pay rates or may take
vacation time at one-half credit for those two days.

Please complete the attached form and return it to your
supervisor no later than April 1.

ytt

Enc. Attachment

Distribution: D. Annabelle
               G. Brokavic
               H. DeAngelo
               P. Frankel
               V. Horowitz
               N. Petruccio
               W. Roberts
               S. Yunez

Practice with plurals, pp. 32-33

1. monopolies	2. highways	3. businesses	4. editors-in-chief
5. currencies	6. bushes	7. bills of lading	8. photocopies
9. passkeys	10. branches		

Practice with possessive forms, pp. 33-34

1. champion's	2. assistants'	3. manager's	4. presidents'
5. supervisor's	6. programmers'	7. users'	8. trainee's
9. staff's	10. receptionists'		

Practice with possessive forms, p. 35

1. A	2. B	3. A	4. A	5. A
6. A	7. A	8. B	9. A	10. A

Mastery Checkpoint One, p. 36

> The faculty*ies* from our three facility*ies* will meet in
> the Erickson Administration Building on Friday
> morning at 10 a.m. The topic will be "Making Media
> Work for You."
>
> J. G. Francis of Future Look Laboratory*ies* will
> demonstrate the latest equipment for educational
> studio*s*: radio*s*, stereos, cameras, and computer
> presentations.
>
> Dr. Francis will also present the results of several
> study*ies* that support the importance of visual aide*s* in
> the classroom.

Mastery Checkpoint Two, p. 36

We have just received an employment application from
Katarina Bortsch, a graduate of Milwaukee's most
prestigious business college. Her skills are
excellent, and she can start in just two week's time.
I am considering her for the administrative assistant
position in Margaret Bush and David Ray's office.

During her interview, Katarina indicated that she had
developed an interest in our company from her
mother's close friend who worked for us in the 1970s.
Both Katarina's academic and personal background
suggest that she would make an excellent employee.

Its been a long time since I have been this impressed
with a candidate. I see the possibility of Katarina
being with us for many years to come.

Formatting practice, p. 47

```
             MEETING OF THE BUILDING DESIGN COMMITTEE
                         Software 4U
                        June 7, 19XX

                          Agenda

     1.  Call to order:  1:30 p.m.

     2.  Approval of minutes from May meeting

     3.  Old business:

         a.  Final action on designs 2 and 3
         b.  Interim action on design 4
         c.  Action on proposal by Landscape
     Architects and Industrial Designers

     4.  New business:

         a.  Planning for architectural design
         b.        Formation of subcommittee

     4.  Adjournment:  3:30 p.m.
```

Practice with frequently misused words, p. 52

1. all right	2. OK	3. lying	4. fewer	5. passed
6. OK	7. stationery	8. affected	9. OK	10. OK
11. quite	12. than	13. complement	14. OK	15. device
16. OK	17. advice	18. OK	19. among	20. OK
21. beside	22. OK	23. further	24. latter	25. may be

Mastery Checkpoint, p. 53

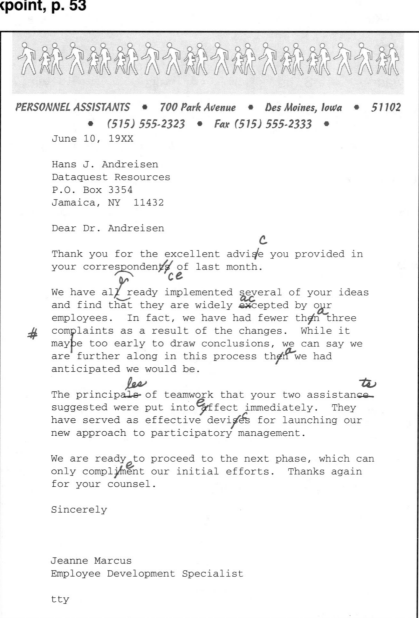

PERSONNEL ASSISTANTS • 700 Park Avenue • Des Moines, Iowa • 51102
• (515) 555-2323 • Fax (515) 555-2333 •

June 10, 19XX

Hans J. Andreisen
Dataquest Resources
P.O. Box 3354
Jamaica, NY 11432

Dear Dr. Andreisen

Thank you for the excellent advi*c*e you provided in your correspondence of last month.

We have all ready implemented several of your ideas and find that they are widely accepted by our employees. In fact, we have had fewer than three complaints as a result of the changes. While it maybe too early to draw conclusions, we can say we are further along in this process than we had anticipated we would be.

The principles of teamwork that your two assistance suggested were put into effect immediately. They have served as effective devices for launching our new approach to participatory management.

We are ready to proceed to the next phase, which can only compliment our initial efforts. Thanks again for your counsel.

Sincerely

Jeanne Marcus
Employee Development Specialist

tty

Agreement practice, p. 70 (top)

1. are	2. look	3. runs	4. meet	5. needs

Agreement practice, p. 70 (bottom)

1. admits   2. is   3. are   4. agree   5. ranks

Agreement practice, p. 71

1. is   2. enjoy   3. is   4. needs   5. is

Agreement practice, p.72

1. are   2. make   3. were   4. ride   5. was

Agreement practice, p. 73

1. was   2. was   3. is   4. sells   5. was

Mastery Checkpoint One, p. 74

1. *line 1*: present, *line 4*: are   2. *line 1*: are, *line 3*: is, *line 4*: is

Mastery Checkpoint Two, p. 74

1. *line 1*: is, *line 3*: is   2. *line 1*: are, *line 3*: does

Formatting practice, p. 87

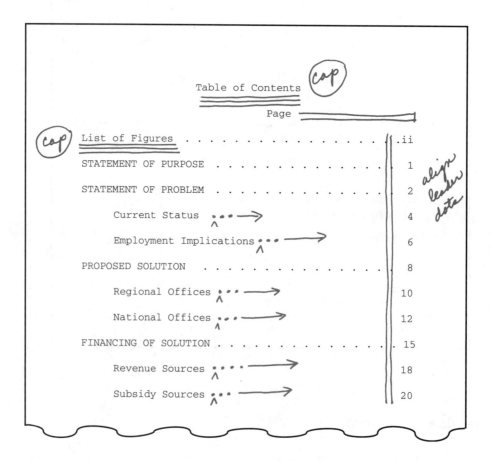

Pronoun practice, pp. 89-90

1. I	2. us	3. her	4. we	5. They
6. him	7. It's	8. us	9. she	10. us

Pronoun practice, p. 91

1. them	2. she	3. me	4. I	5. he
6. she	7. she	8. I	9. I	10. they

Pronoun practice, p. 93

1. his	2. they	3. their	4. their	5. its

Parallelism practice, p. 94
Note: Solutions may vary.

1. Send a copy of the letter both to John Avery and Iva Gray.
2. My new duties include preparing the accounts, balancing the worksheets, and budgets. *[preparing]* *[promising]*
3. Neither improving her skills nor a promise to arrive on time will save her job at this point.
4. Alison not only wrote the report but also is typing it. *[typed]*
5. The subheadings of the report are:

   Determining Our Purpose
   Refining Our Goals *[-ing]*
   Achievement of Our Goals

Mastery Checkpoint One, p. 94
Note: Solutions may vary.

1. The state negotiator agreed to meet with the union officers
   (1.) and I on May 1. (2.) Its imperative that you and I meet before
   that date. I know you want this issue resolved as much as
   (3.) me. Since it was (4.) them who requested the meeting, I think the
   possibility is good.

   (1.) me   (3.) I
   (2.) It's   (4.) they

2. Dean gave the report to Carlita and (1.) I on Friday. Carlita
   hopes to meet with (2.) he and Mr. Weinstein (3.) on Monday. Do
   you think you could attend rather than me? Just between
   you and (4.) I, I think you are better informed about the matter.

   (1.) me   (3.) I
   (2.) him   (4.) me

Mastery Checkpoint Two, p. 95
Note: Solutions may vary.

1. The committee has decided to review their findings on the environmental impact of the testing. Each of the members is to review his own position. Everyone is to then submit the results of their second review to Sandi Kyte.

   (1.) *its*

   (2.) *his or her*

   (3.) *the*

2. Each doctor on staff performs in his own unique manner. Likewise, each nurse brings her own personality to the job. The result is a team that functions very smoothly. Everyone can be proud that he is a member of the Sunrise team!

   (1.) *a (or his or her)*

   (2.) *his or her*

   (3.) *to be*

Mastery Checkpoint Three, p. 95
Note: Solutions may vary.

1. The supervisor was having difficulty deciding whether he should promote Elizabeth Cantor or to transfer her to another department. Greeting people is one of her strengths but to file accurately is one of her weaknesses.

   (1.) *or transfer (delete to)*

   (2.) *filing*

2. The consultants studied the proposals and how they were developed. The process included conducting a needs assessment, setting program goals, and measurement of outcomes.

   (1.) *their development*

   (2.) *measuring*

Formatting practice, p. 104

```
the task of making a newsletter readable.  Most
readers like lots of white space, lots of graphics, a
```

Page 10 _____ ↓ ½" *from bottom*
⌐OR⌐

join to beginning of word →

George Kovale   September 15, 19XX   Page 2

ts
(r)upted plans for the next meeting are incomplete.
Ashley will call you when she has further
information.

Adjective practice, p. 106

1. brighter 2. more 3. best 4. more 5. hardest

Adjective practice, p. 107
Note: Answers may vary.

1. Supplies are ~~more~~ cheaper at Office Biz.
OK 2. Our goal is to do a more complete study next year.
3. The new fountain in the courtyard is ~~more~~ taller than the old one.
4. The meeting was definitely ~~more~~ shorter than the previous one.
5. Your opinion is the least ~~kindest~~ I have heard.

Verb practice, p. 108

1. spoken 2. begun 3. gone 4. did 5. hidden

Mastery Checkpoint One, p. 109

1. I have just completed the review of the ~~most~~ finest sales
   campaign we have ever conducted. Of the top two
   territories, Midwest and Mountain Plains, the Midwest had
   ~~the most~~ sales. Of the next three territories, the South had
   ~~more~~ sales.

   ① *delete most*   ③ *the most*
   ② *more*

2. Which of you has the ~~highest~~ (1.) salary? I need to do a ~~more~~ (2.) total review of everyone's salary history. Since you are two of the ~~more older~~ (3.) employees, I think you are a good starting point. Is it ~~best~~ (4.) to interview you or to conduct a review of your records?

(1.) *higher*   (3.) *oldest*
(2.) *delete more*   (4.) *better*

Mastery Checkpoint Two, p. 109

1. The technicians have ~~came~~ (1.) three times this week and have ~~did~~ (2.) their best to correct the "bug" in our systems. We have ~~began~~ (3.) to think the problem cannot be corrected. We are very disappointed because these computers were carefully ~~chose~~ (4.) after comparison shopping.

(1.) *come*   (3.) *begun*
(2.) *done*   (4.) *chosen*

2. Public Act 489 has ~~laid~~ (1.) on Lucinda Dey's congresswoman's desk for more than 90 days. Lucinda Dey has ~~wrote~~ (2.) to her expressing her feelings in the matter. She is so incensed she wishes she had ~~flew~~ (3.) to Washington on her recent business trip to Philadelphia.

(1.) *lain*   (3.) *flown*
(2.) *written*

Formatting practice, p. 119

Punctuation practice, p. 121

1. Will you respond as quickly as possible to my letter.
2. C. A. Brownson, M.D., is our guest lecturer.
3. The stock exchanges are commonly referred to as the N.Y.S.E., the A.M.E.X., and the N.A.S.D.A.Q.
4. I. Primary Computer Printers
   A. Dot-matrix
   B. Letter-quality
   II. Optical Character Readers
5. Leslie asked if our present insurance program was adequate.

Punctuation practice, p. 122

1. When will the first draft be ready for review?
2. Congratulations on your promotion!
3. Where is our next seminar scheduled?
4. Tell me: What is the current status of the study?
5. Unbelievable! How else can I describe it?

Punctuation practice, p. 123

1. Ralph has proven to be a dedicated, responsible department supervisor.
2. Our group is meeting tomorrow morning, and we will resolve the problem of lower production levels.
3. The agenda includes employee absenteeism, low morale, and negative work attitudes.
4. Send your reply in the stamped, self-addressed envelope.
5. The minutes of the meeting are ready, and they will be distributed tomorrow.

Punctuation practice, p. 125

1. Our corporate librarian, Christine Blews, M.L.S., was nominated for an outstanding literary award.
2. After I complete my degree, I intend to apply for the management development program.
3. Am I correct, Cynthia, that you designed this month's newsletter?
4. I will take my vacation when the project is completed.
5. Passing the state bar exam, which is my immediate goal, will enable me to fulfill a lifelong dream.
ok 6. Xydec Inc. will be the major supplier.
7. Sara Greenstein and Lynn Resnick, Jr., have been chosen "Employees of the Month."

Punctuation practice, p. 126

1. Those present were Roger Babcock, chairperson; Loren Balyeat, secretary; and Diane Faw, controller.
2. We did not purchase the Superior computers; however, we will reconsider the bid for the new division.
3. Ergonomics is an important consideration; a task force has been appointed to prepare a status report on the topic.
4. While we intend to introduce a graphics package soon, we are concentrating on other peripherals; but we will keep you informed on the progress of the proposed software.
5. Teresa McCandless, my immediate supervisor, has asked me to chair the committee; and I have willingly accepted the challenge.

Punctuation practice, p. 127

> The fifth-floor supervisor suggested that the following issues be included in the discussion: relocation of all furniture, purchase of new furniture, or a combination of the two—her particular preference. For your information, the idea of making the move on Saturday was rejected by a two-thirds vote of those involved.

Mastery Checkpoint One, p. 128

1. Will you please mark July 10 on your calendar now? That is the date we have chosen for our company picnic. We are looking for volunteers for three committees:

   1. Promotion
   2. Entertainment
   3. Food and Beverages

2. I can't believe you did that! Didn't you think of the long-term effects of your recent action? That could have serious consequences for your future in the organization; don't you think? Marissa asked if you could meet in her office at 9 a.m. tomorrow to discuss the situation.

Mastery Checkpoint Two, p. 128

1. It is our intent to study the following areas, human resources, finance and long-range planning. When the study is completed the task-force will prepare a comprehensive, up-to-date summary.

2. On the new system you can access online libraries, newspapers, encyclopedias, bulletin boards, banking services and more, these will all be at your fingertips. This is an exciting development.

Proofreading envelopes, p. 130

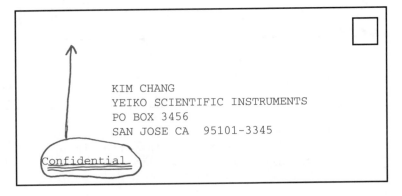

KIM CHANG
YEIKO SCIENTIFIC INSTRUMENTS
PO BOX 3456
SAN JOSE CA   95101-3345

Confidential

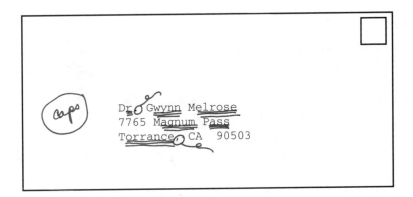

caps

Dr. Gwynn Melrose
7765 Magnum Pass
Torrance, CA   90503

CITIZEN MUTUAL INSURANCE GROUP
420 LEXINGTON AVENUE
NEW YORK ~~NEW YORK~~ 1170   *missing digit*
NY

Formatting practice, p. 139

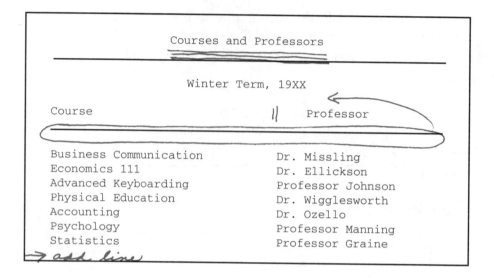

```
                        Courses and Professors


                        Winter Term, 19XX

        Course                       Professor


        Business Communication       Dr. Missling
        Economics 111                Dr. Ellickson
        Advanced Keyboarding         Professor Johnson
        Physical Education           Dr. Wigglesworth
        Accounting                   Dr. Ozello
        Psychology                   Professor Manning
        Statistics                   Professor Graine
```

add line

Capitalization practice, p. 141

```
        the article began:  "the only decision more difficult
than choosing a computer is selecting the right
printer." you may choose from two types:  impact and
nonimpact your final decision should be based on
your needs
```

Capitalization practice, p. 142

```
    Our new satellite office, located on the East side
of Exeter Boulevard in the great Southwest city of
Santa Fe, New Mexico, is having its grand opening on
April 23, 19XX. Mark Ewing, Professor of Endocrinology
and President-Elect of the local University faculty
group, will give the keynote address. Platform guests
should meet in the second floor conference room at
1:30 p.m.
```

Capitalization practice, p. 144

delete
underscore
set in
ital

```
    We found the chapter "A Positive Approach To
Conflict Management," in Author Tustin's new book,
SUCCESSFUL NEGOTIATIONS, very helpful in resolving
the differences between the Accounting and Corporate
Audit departments. Joanna Glancy and Norton Holmes,
the respective Department Managers, applied the
Author's approach to their situation and are very
happy with the results.
```

Mastery Checkpoint One, p. 145

1. The chairman of the board announced: "we are very pleased to announce the acquisition of the following properties:
   1. the Southwest corner of Phoenix and Grand Streets
   2. a 2-acre plot just East of our present site on Ramada Avenue
   3. the former home of Senator-Elect Murphy"

2. The renovation of the Third Floor Employee Cafeteria has begun. The details of funding for this project are in the August Minutes of the OOC.

Mastery Checkpoint Two, p. 145

1. The community group in the City was very eager to hear the newly elected Mayor present his plan for neighborhood renewal. These people are a dynamic group of activists; Mayor Laverty pledged the full support of his Administration to their efforts.

2. Brian Gimbel, author of YOU CAN MAKE A DIFFERENCE!, had the group on the edge of their seats. As a former Director within the U.S. Department of Justice and Chairman of Employee Relations, he certainly has the background to understand today's business environment.

Formatting practice, p. 156

Title should be in all caps; need unit numbers on the vertical axis; bars are not proportionate (do not reflect the numbers).

Practice with numbers, p. 158

1. We have only 8 sample items left.
2. Margaret gained twenty-five new customers last month.
3. Please repaint all 10 doors.
4. You should have shipped 37 dictionaries, nine word books, and 3 thesauruses.
5. I have one check but 12 deposit slips remaining.

Practice with numbers, p. 159

> 67 *(sp out)* sales representatives have already confirmed their plans to attend the annual sales *(sp out)* conference to be held at our corporate headquarters, ① Fifth Avenue, New York City. We expect a total attendance of 200, which is three-fourths of our staff. We have already reserved 210 ② room suites at the prestigious Hotel Barclay. *(sp out)*

Practice with numbers, p. 160
Note: Answers for question 5 may vary; consistency is the goal.

1. The deposit included three items: $50 .00, currency; $12.50, coins; and $75 .00, checks.
2. Since our warehouse space is limited, please ship ~~fifty~~ 50 thirty-lb. bags. *or fifty 30-lb.*
3. Is the middle number of your social security number ~~thirty-one~~ 31 or ~~thirteen~~ 13?
4. Our new address is Suite ~~Fifteen~~ 15 in the new Pueblo Medical Center.
5. The progressive rates are 3%, 4%, and 4.75 percent. *or %*

Practice with numbers, p. 162
Note: Answers may vary; consistency is the goal.

> Angela Swarthmore, whom we hired on July 15~~th~~ last year, travels coast to coast several times a month. She is still fascinated by the fact that she can leave New York's LaGuardia Airport at 9 o'clock and arrive in Los Angeles at 11:30 A. M., just in time for lunch. On her recent trip she celebrated her thirty-fifth birthday. On the twenty-third of August she will make her first trans-Atlantic flight. That date also marks the ~~3rd~~ *third* anniversary of her joining the company.

Mastery Checkpoint One, p. 162

1. Our order clearly stated "17 plotter cartridges in assorted colors"; we received only ~~seven~~ 7, all red. Please ship the remaining 10 in assorted colors (other than red) via Express Mail to our home office at ① Madison Avenue. *(sp out)*

2. ~~Two thousand forty-three~~ *by 2,043* respondents agree that our Tel-desk disks are *rated* the best on the market. This year we have already shipped 7,115 10-disk cartons (or 1/10 of all disks sold) to leading computer dealers. *(sp out)*

Mastery Checkpoint Two, p. 162

1. Please check the correctness of our Invoice No. ~~Four Hundred Five~~ *405* . The correct price on the binders is $4.75 not ~~$~~ 7.45; the correct price on fillers is $1.23 not *$* 1.32. The correct discount for prompt payment should be 3.5 ~~percent~~ , not 3% . *percent*

2. If you print your brochure on ~~twenty~~ *20-* lb. bond paper, you will increase its usefulness. We can have the finished copies for you next Friday, April 15th. Call me after 9 o'clock that morning, and we will arrange delivery.

Formatting practice, p. 173
Note: Some answers may vary.

1. Select a sans serif typeface for the heading.
2. Set the heading in a larger type size.
3. Select a serif typeface for the text.
4. Add space between paragraphs.
5. Consider using a ragged-right margin.

Sentence structure practice, p. 175
Note: These are suggested edits; answers may vary.

1. Jan and Kerry attended the seminar; they found it very helpful.
2. Her promotion was unexpected at this time, since it was not part of her performance review.
3. ~~Even though~~ I am in total disagreement with you.
4. We will be happy to review your proposal if you will provide us with a complete description of the final product.
5. The team concept was not successful; few of our employees understood it.

Sentence structure practice, pp. 176-177
Note: These are suggested edits; answers may vary.

1. *When she was* Stepping from the elevator, the door closed on her foot.
2. Enclosed are two receipts for ~~merchandise~~ you have not received previously.
3. George's and Kevin's budgets were denied because ~~he~~ *they* refused to include a 3 percent cut in overhead.
4. She only gets two weeks' vacation.
5. As our newest employee, it is my privilege to welcome you aboard.

Mastery Checkpoint, p. 177
Note: These are suggested edits; answers may vary.

1. Today I learned that Sharon Vincenzo and Elayne Crippen were suspended for insubordinate behavior. Can you verify whether ~~she~~ *either* plans to take legal action?

2. The network will be installed next Monday, Which explains why we are not inputting this data until late next week. Francine Georges will work with our technicians for the next two weeks, they will find her to be a very competent trainer.

Formatting practice, p. 183
Note: These are suggested edits; answers may vary.

1. Your order #345 will be shipped on Monday, March 17, via Midwest Trucking.
2. We have the following dates open: Monday, January 15; Tuesday, January 16; and Wednesday, January 17.
3. Your job performance over the past six months has not been up to its usual level.
4. Helen Jackson of our Customer Service Division will investigate the concerns you raised.
5. Since this change represents such a different perspective, how do you think it will be accepted by the group?

Concise wording practice, p. 185
Note: These are suggested edits; answers may vary.

1. The purpose of the meeting is to review the tentative labor agreement.
2. Thank you for your cooperation.
3. Please send the confirmation separately.
4. Enclosed is your corrected statement. Please pay the amount due as soon as possible.
5. Since our expanded facilities will not be complete until August, we cannot purchase office furniture now.

Concise wording practice, p. 186
Note: These are suggested edits; answers may vary.

1. The alternative is to revert to our original production method.
2. The consensus is that the facts may never be known.
3. Our priority is to use experience to solve the problem.
4. The new warehouse should be finished by June 15.
5. The meeting will give you an opportunity to express your feelings about the issue.

Mastery Checkpoint, p. 187
Note: This is suggested editing; answers may vary.

```
Ladies and Gentlemen:

Thank you for your letter regarding your past due
account. We have checked all of the last year's
transactions and have been unable to locate the
amount in question.

We think the amount was simply entered twice.  Could
you send us the invoice number of the transaction?

As soon as I receive this, we will settle the matter
quickly because you are one of our valued customers.

Thank you.

Sincerely,
```

Sample opening paragraph, p. 191

Choice 2 is preferred because it is concise. It contains all necessary information without added words.

Sample supporting paragraph, p. 191

Choice 1 is preferred because it is concise and gives the reader specific information.

Sample closing paragraph, p. 191

Choice 1 is preferred because it refers the reader to a specific person for assistance.

Practice with details, pp. 193-194

1. Date is missing.   2. Room location is missing.   3. No location is indicated.

Mastery Checkpoint, p. 195

Note: Suggested editing includes eliminating wordiness. While answers may vary, the important task for this exercise is to notice missing or inaccurate details.

```
     MEMORANDUM


     TO:        Marvin Gottlieb
                Jennifer Doran

     FROM:      Clarence McDevitt

     DATE:      July 7, 19xx

     SUBJECT:   MONTHLY REPORT FORMAT
                                                        *1000 11?
     As of today, I have received monthly reports from (1) of our
     16 departments. I have found that each of these requires
     three to four hours to review due to inconsistency of format.

     To be specific:
                                                                    *10 listed
     * Departments 1, 3, 5, and 7 used our new report                 here
       software.            followed
     * Departments 2, 4, 6, 8, 9, and 10 did not use the
       new software and prepared the reports according to
       individual preferences. in formatting
     For efficiency
     I like to give personnel every opportunity to adjust to
     changes on their own. However, I must insist that the new
     software be installed and used, effective immediately.

     To facilitate this, I am scheduling a second users' workshop
     for two weeks from today, July 28. Each department must send
     the appropriate person(s) to
     this workshop.

     bxm
```

I. SPELLING

The Silent *e*

1. Drop the silent *e* when adding a suffix beginning with a vowel.
2. Retain the silent *e* when adding a suffix beginning with a consonant.
3. Retain the silent *e* when adding a suffix to a word ending in *ee*.

ie or *ei*?

4. Use *i* before *e* except after *c*; or when sounded like *a* as in *neighbor* or *weigh*.

Common exceptions	height, foreign, leisure

ie or *y*?

5. When a word ends in *y* preceded by a consonant, change the *y* to *i* and add the suffix.
6. When a word ends in *y* preceded by a vowel, do not change the *y* to *i*; add the suffix to the base word.

Common exceptions	lay ⇨ laid, pay ⇨ paid, say ⇨ said

7. When a word ends in *ie*, change the *ie* to *y* before adding *ing*.

Final Consonants

8. *Do not* double a final consonant if the suffix begins with a consonant.
9. When the word has two or more syllables and the accent is on the second syllable, *do* double the final consonant before adding the suffix.

Troublesome Word Endings

10. ible/able

    Three tips will help you add the correct ending to these words:

    - *able* is the more commonly used ending
    - *able* is usually added to complete words
    - *ible* is usually added to incomplete words

Ible usually follows syllables ending in *ss*, such as access + ible = accessible.

11. <u>ceed/cede/sede</u>

Three tips will help you master these:

- *cede* is the most frequently used ending
- only three words end in *ceed*: proceed, exceed, and succeed
- only one word ends in *sede*: supersede

12. <u>ery/ary</u>

Knowing that *ary* is the more common ending will help you.

13. <u>ize/ise/yse</u>

There are over ten times as many words ending in *ize* as in *ise*.

Only one commonly used word ends in *yze*: analyze.

II. PLURALS

1. Most plurals are formed by simply adding *s* to the singular form of the word.
2. When the noun ends in *s, x, z, ch*, or *sh*, add *es*.
3. When the noun ends in *y* preceded by a *vowel*, simply add an *s*.
4. When the noun ends in *y* preceded by a *consonant*, change the *y* to *ie* and add *s*.
5. When a noun ends in *fe*, generally change the *fe* to *ve* and add *s*.
6. When the noun ends in *o*, generally add *s*.
7. Add the plural to the main word of compound expressions and hyphenated words.

III. POSSESSIVES

<u>Common Formation of Possessives</u>

1. The possessive of nouns is formed in one of two ways:

- By adding '*s* to most singular nouns: *employee* becomes *employee's*

- By adding ' to most plural nouns: *employees* becomes *employees'*

2. The possessive form is used for pronouns showing possession.

Troublesome Possessives

3. When two nouns share ownership, only the second noun is possessive.
4. When two nouns have separate ownership, both nouns are possessive.
5. The possessive of some common plural words is always formed by adding *'s*.
6. The possessive of units of time follows a simple guideline:

   - When referring to one unit of time, add *'s*.
   - When referring to two or more units of time, add *s'*.

7. The possessive form is usually used before a *gerund*, a verb ending in *ing* acting as a noun.

IV. SUBJECT-VERB AGREEMENT

Agreement in Number

1. The subject and verb must always agree in number.

   - A singular subject must have a singular verb.
   - A plural subject must have a plural verb.

Compound Subjects

2. Subjects joined by *and* require plural verbs.
3. Singular subjects joined by *or* require singular verbs.
4. If a singular subject and a plural subject are joined by *or* or *nor*, the verb agrees in number with the subject closer to it.

Agreement of Pronouns and Verbs

5. When a subject is preceded by *each* or *every*, the verb is always singular.
6. Indefinite pronouns are always followed by singular verbs.

7. The pronoun *you* is always followed by a plural verb.
8. The expression, "A number," requires a plural verb; the epression, "The number," takes a singular verb.

Find the Subject

9. <u>There and here</u>. *There* and *here* are adverbs and, as such, are never the subject of the sentence. Look for the subject elsewhere in the sentence.
10. <u>Intervening words</u>. One of the most confusing choices in agreement is having to select the verb when words come between the subject and the verb. Sometimes these are explanatory and may be in the form of a prepositional phrase. Again, you must find the simple subject and make certain that the simple subject and verb agree in number. Intervening phrases never determine the verb.

Collective Nouns

11. Nouns that name a group are called *collective nouns*. Since collective nouns refer to the group as a whole, they are usually singular.
12. Proper nouns ending in *s* may appear plural. Usually, however, they are singular.

V. PRONOUNS

The Correct Case

1. <u>Nominative case</u>. The *nominative case* is used in two ways:

   * When the pronoun is the subject
   * When the pronoun follows a linking verb: *is, are, am, was, were, be,* and *been*

2. <u>Objective case</u>. The *objective case* pronouns are *me, us, you, him, her, it, them, whom*. The objective case is used in two ways:

   * When the pronoun is the object of a verb
   * When the pronoun is the object of a preposition

   Remember that the object answers the question "who" or "what" after the verb.

3. <u>Possessive case</u>. Do *not* use an apostrophe with a possessive pronoun. The possessive case is used to show ownership.

Using Pronouns with Compounds and after *Than* or *As*

4. Nominative case pronouns are used as subjects or predicate nominatives; objective case pronouns are used as objects of verbs or prepositions.
5. When a personal pronoun follows the word *as* or *than*, choose the correct case by mentally inserting the missing words.

Agreement in Number and Gender

6. A pronoun must agree in number and gender with its antecedent.
7. Formerly the masculine gender was used when the antecedent applied to persons of both sexes. That practice is no longer considered acceptable. Instead, do one of the following:

   • Use both masculine and feminine gender pronouns.
   • Change the antecedent and pronoun from singular to plural.
   • Rewrite the sentence to avoid the use of a pronoun.

Indefinite Pronouns and Compound Antecedents

8. Some indefinite pronouns are singular: *each, every, either, neither, one, another,* and *much.*
9. When a prepositional phrase follows an indefinite pronoun, the prepositional phrase is not the antecedent and, therefore, does not determine the number of the pronoun.
10. When two or more antecedents are joined by the word *and*, a plural pronoun is used.

VI. PARALLELISM

Related items should be grammatically consistent. This is referred to as *parallel structure* or *parallelism*.

VII. ADJECTIVES

Comparative and Superlative Forms

1. Comparative Form

   Generally form the comparative by adding *er* or *more/less* to the adjective.

   Use the comparative form when comparing two things.

2. Superlative Form

   Generally form the superlative by adding *est* or *most/least* to the adjective.

   Use the superlative form when comparing three or more things.

Troublesome Comparisons

3. Avoid double comparisons.

   Wrong: Your diet is the *most* healthi*est* I have ever known.
   Right: Your diet is the healthi*est* I have ever known.

   Some adjectives should not be compared: round, full.

VIII. VERBS

1. *Regular verbs* form the past tense and past participle by adding *d* or *ed*.

Present tense	Past tense	Past participle
employ	employed	employed

2. *Irregular verbs* form the past tense and past participle by changing form.

Present tense	Past tense	Past participle
see	saw	seen

   The past participle must *always* have a helping verb. A helping verb is an auxiliary word: *is, are, am, was, were, has, have, had, can, could, do, did, may, might, must, shall, will, should,* and *could.*

Past tense: I *saw* the doctor twice last week.
Past participle: I *have seen* the doctor twice in the last week.

IX. PUNCTUATION

Periods

1. A period is used to end complete thoughts, including courteous requests and indirect questions (paraphrases of the actual question).
2. Periods are used within initials, academic degrees, and many abbreviations.
3. Do not use a period in abbreviated organization names and acronyms.
4. Use periods after letters or numbers in outlines and lists.

Question Marks and Exclamation Points

5. Use a question mark after a direct question.
6. Use a question mark at the end of a statement that contains a direct question.
7. Use an exclamation point to express strong feeling or emotion.

Commas with Independent Clauses, Series, and Coordinate Adjectives

8. Use a comma to separate two independent clauses joined by a conjunction.
9. Use a comma to separate the items in a series. It is common business practice to use the comma before the conjunction in a series.
10. Two adjectives modifying the same noun are called *coordinate adjectives*. Use a comma to separate coordinate adjectives.

Commas with Phrases and Clauses

11. Use a comma with interrupting words, phrases, and clauses.
12. Use a comma to set off nonessential modifiers.
13. Omit the comma before or after essential modifiers.
14. Use a comma to set off words of direct address.

Commas with Personal and Company Abbreviations

15. Use commas to set off a person's professional position or educational degree.
16. The trend is to eliminate commas setting off personal and company abbreviations that are part of the name.

Semicolons

17. Use a semicolon to replace a conjunction in a compound sentence. The following sentence is written two ways to help you understand this.

Compound sentence with a conjunction:

The tests have been given, *and* the results have been posted.

Same sentence with a semicolon replacing the conjunction:

The tests have been given; the results have been posted.

18. Use a semicolon when a compound sentence is very long or already contains commas.
19. When one part of a compound sentence contains a comma because of a transitional phrase, use a semicolon to separate the parts.
20. When a series already has internal commas, use a semicolon between the parts of the series to enhance readability.

Colons

21. Use a colon to introduce lists and enumerations.
22. Use a colon to introduce long quotations.

Hyphens

23. Hyphens are used to join *compound adjectives*—two adjectives forming one idea—*before* a noun.
24. Hyphens are used in a series of compound adjectives modifying the same noun.

Dashes

25. Use a dash to indicate an abrupt break in thought or to add an afterthought. Careful writers use dashes sparingly.

X. CAPITALIZATION

First Words

1. Capitalize the first word of a full-sentence quotation.
2. Capitalize the first word after a colon only when a complete sentence follows.
3. Capitalize the first words in listed items when the items are designated by letters, numbers, or other symbols.
4. Capitalize the first words in sections of formal outlines.
5. Capitalize each major word in a salutation but only the first word in a closing.

Proper Nouns

6. Capitalize proper nouns and proper adjectives.
7. Capitalize only those parts of hyphenated terms that are proper nouns or adjectives.
8. Capitalize geographical place names and regions.
9. Capitalize days of the week, months, and holidays.
10. Capitalize words that precede or are designated by numbers when they represent complete titles or labels. Do not capitalize partial or common labels.

Titles

11. Capitalize titles that precede or are part of a person's name.
12. Do not capitalize a title if the name is set off by commas.
13. Generally do not capitalize occupational or other titles such as *manager, consultant, mother,* or *grandfather.*
14. Capitalize a title when used in direct address.
15. Capitalize the names of committees and departments when they are the official names.
16. Capitalize major words in names of government bodies and official organizations.
17. Capitalize all major words in titles of written or performed works.
18. Capitalize brand names but not the products themselves.

Subject Lines and Headings

19. The subject line of memos may appear in all caps, initial caps, or boldface.
20. Side headings in reports may appear in all caps or with initial caps (underlining optional).
21. Book titles may be typed in all caps, italicized, or underscored.

XI. NUMBERS

Figures or Words?

1. Numbers one through ten are spelled out; numbers over ten are written as figures.
2. Related numbers should be consistent. If related items contain figures above and below ten, the usual practice is to list all items in figures.

Numbers Expressed as Words

3. Numbers beginning a sentence. These should always be spelled out. If the number is large, it is a good practice to rearrange the sentence.
4. Addresses. Numbered street names one through ten are spelled out.
   A house or building address of *One* is spelled out.

Two Numbers Appearing Together

5. When two related numbers appear together, generally spell out the smaller one.
6. If two unrelated numbers appear together, separate them by a comma.

Fractions Standing Alone

7. Fractions standing alone within text are spelled out.

Numbers Expressed as Figures

8. Amounts of money. Sums of money are always written in figures.

   Amounts of money less than one dollar are written in figures followed by *cents*.

   Even dollar amounts are not followed by a decimal and zeros unless other related items include cents.

9. Measurements and other specifications. Numbers used as measurements, sizes, temperatures, dimensions, and identification numbers always appear in figures.
10. Percentages. In business correspondence, the amount of a percentage is stated in figures followed by the word *percent*.
11. Numbers following nouns. When a number follows a descriptor such as *Chapter, Volume, Room, Model,* or *page,* it is expressed in figures.
12. Numbers in compound adjectives. Numbers in compound adjectives appear in figures.

Numbers in Dates and Times

13. Dates. The date is always written in figures when it follows the month.

    Dates expressed as ordinal numbers (5th or fifth) are *only* used when the day precedes the month.

14. Time. While time designations using *a.m.* or *p.m.* are preferred, it is also correct in some instances to use *o'clock.*

    The expression *o'clock* is generally used with words such as *tonight, in the afternoon,* and so on. When used, the time is always spelled out.

    Times of day followed by a.m. or p.m. are expressed in figures.

XII. SENTENCE STRUCTURE

Fragments and Run-ons

1. Use grammatically complete sentences in your writing, except in the least formal situations. Incomplete sentences are called *sentence fragments.*
2. A second type of faulty sentence structure is a *run-on sentence*—two or more sentences punctuated as a single sentence.

Modifiers

3. Place modifiers as close as possible to the words they modify.
4. Make certain your modifiers serve as clear references.

XIII. CONCISE WORDING

Excessive Wording and Outdated Expressions

1. Avoid overused and dated words and expressions.

Excessive wording	Concise wording
at this point in time	now
can be in a position to	can
due to the fact that	because
each and every one	every one
for the purpose of	for
in a position to	can
in the near future	soon
inasmuch as	since
make inquiry regarding	ask about
meets with our approval	we approve
our experience indicated	we learned

Outdated expressions	Concise wording
at your earliest convenience	soon
Dear Sirs	Gentlemen
Dear Sirs and Madams	Ladies and Gentlemen
enclosed please find	enclosed is
in receipt of	have
thanking you for	thank you
thank you in advance	thank you
under separate cover	separately

Redundancies

2. Avoid redundant expressions in both spoken and written language.

The following list of common redundancies will help increase your awareness. Note that only the italicized word is needed.

advance *planning*	new *innovation*
basic *fundamentals*	*revert (refer)* back
completely *finished*	true *facts*
past *experience*	

INDEX

PROOFREADER'S CUE CARD

Mark	Meaning	Example	Corrected
‖	Align vertically	A positive attitude makes the day go faster.	A positive attitude makes the day go faster.
⌒	Close up	over head projector	overhead projector
(delete) (or)	Delete text	Maria and and Juan	Maria and Juan
		committment	commitment
———	Delete and replace text	*will* I shall plan to do so.	I will plan to do so.
}}	Delete justification	Your job interview is next Monday at 2:30 p.m.	Your job interview is next Monday at 2:30 p.m.
SS|DS|TS	Correct line spacing (single space, double space, triple space)	SS employers, employees, and consultants	employers, employees, and consultants
⊏	Move left	after the meeting	after the meeting
⊐	Move right	1.BASIC 2. FORTRAN 3. Assembly	1. BASIC 2. FORTRAN 3. Assembly
(move)	Move text	She only mailed it yesterday.	She mailed it only yesterday.
¶	New paragraph	¶ Your report is due.	Your report is due.
no ¶	No paragraph	The check is in the mail. no ¶ Please call me when you receive it.	The check is in the mail. Please call me when you receive it.
⊐⊏	Center	⊐Agenda⊏	Agenda
∧	Insert text	*new* the person	the new person
⌄	Insert punctuation	phones, tapes and TVs	phones, tapes, and TVs
#	Insert space	phones,tapes, and TVs	phones, tapes, and TVs
———	Underline	Requirement #1	Requirement #1

Some proofreaders' marks that use margin notations are illustrated here.

Marks Text/Margin	Meaning	Example	Corrected
⬭ (sp)	Spell out	Liz J. McKenna (sp)	Elizabeth J. McKenna
⋂ (tr)	Transpose (switch)	reciept (tr)	receipt
⁓⁓⁓ (bf)	Set in boldface	WORLD CHAMPIONS (bf)	**WORLD CHAMPIONS**
⬭ (lf)	Set in lightface	the expression OK (lf)	the expression OK
≡ (Caps)	Add caps	fbi (Caps)	FBI
⌐ (lc)	Use lower case	WASHINGTON (lc)	Washington
.... (stet)	Leave as is	*typewriting* keyboarding (stet)	keyboarding
⬭ (wf)	Wrong font (type style)	the (wf)	the
——— (ital)	Add italics	vis-a-vis (ital)	*vis-a-vis*